AF335454

Reflections OF US

a collection of verse

THOMAS HIMES

Contents

*"Everything and everyone who shows up in our lives
is a reflection of something that is happening inside of
us,"* Alan Cohen

Introduction

One evening before this book was published, I was discussing it at dinner with our family. My son-in-law, a rather inquisitive, perceptive fella, asked me where I got inspiration for the poems.

I didn't think much about it, responding with the f rst thing that came to mind, "Oh, I don't know, they just come to me." Later I thought, "Of course they do, as everything I write does." But there is more to it, much more. "Why do the ideas and thoughts come to me and where do they come from?"

In a more contemplative mood sometime later, I pondered those questions and wished I could have recreated the moment of missed opportunity for a more authentic answer.

I would have said the true Inspiration for this work is from the script of my life from childhood, a script written by others for a role I played on the stage of a life of loss and dysfunction, which would take me far from the truth of who I was born to be. It was only through discovery of a new script, a spiritual journey back to that truth, that I would regain the wholeness to share my words with others.

The spiritual journey has given me an appreciation for the oneness of life, each of us much more alike than we are different. And yet within the oneness, we retain a uniqueness of ourselves.

It is from this realization, "Refl ections of Us, a collection of verse," has come to be. Each verse is a ref ection, something of myself I see in everyone and everything I experience, my inner child in my grandson as a toddler (Walking Boys), the beauty of my wife's eyes (Blue Eyes) illness of my father (Troubled Man), sacred land (Sacred Spirit), and even in tragedy (Where Was God).

The poems, for the most part, are in the order they were written. The subjects are diverse, a variety of matter from observations over a very long period of my life. Collectively, they are best described as spiritual, earthy, powerful, and entertaining.

Each poem before you a mirror my friend to reflect upon, so take your time, no hurry of course, simply sit awhile on the bench of us to see what is reflecting back.

The Great Poet

One day and far away the Great Poet
of the universe scratched his head and
exclaimed, "Today I'll write a masterpiece
for all creation to enjoy."

And so, in the early morning before the
dew had dried on the eternal grass, he
took pen in hand, retired to his garden and
with a finger beside his head began.

He thought and thought and thought
some more, the words then spilled out in
a special verse for all those he'd created,
the seeds of his love to surely grow in the
garden of each heart.

And most important he thought those who
share the planet would learn to see not the
differences in their brothers and sisters but
the oneness of them reflecting back.

*Let's see, he thought, how about a touch
of encouragement for those trying so hard
to make life happen, for them I'll prescribe
a new idea to try, to take it easy and just
let me be in charge.*

*Next, he thought, I must administer a special
stanza for all the mothers this day who
nurture and care for those they hold dear.*

*He brushed aside a tear when he thought
of the sons and daughters who had gone
to war and not returned and quickly
penned a special verse to ease the pain of
the mothers and fathers here at home.*

*And for the homeless, which he knew were
so many, he smiled with an idea of finding
some new words to describe not their
plight but possibilities of a better life.*

*Then his hand turned the page and
he had to chuckle knowing dawn was
soon to come, darkness to subside and
summoned a large share of his love for all
those of creation who would awaken to a
new day.*

*Let's see, he thought, where else at this
time might I proclaim my writing pen
ready and able its ink to paint a picture
of freedom from bondage, I believe I'll
declare right here and now, wherever it be,
it is their right given by me.*

*And then in closing he wrote some words
for those who feel they never have enough
of life's pleasures and sustenance to heed
the words his son had said of coming to
bring life more abundantly to change their
thinking.*

*Then the day arrived he believed he was
done, he heard himself say, "Not so fast,"
there's one more verse to write of the
doctors, nurses and first responders, my
special angels assigned to care for the
sick and the wounded who go about their
tasks with love in their hearts.*

*When he'd written of encouragement, new
mothers, sons and daughters off to war,
the homeless, freedom and those in the
healing professions, he took leave of the
task declaring all he wrote perfect for then
but vowed to return the next day and every
day thereafter to write another verse of
those he loved.*

What You See

What do you see when you look at me, is it me you see or a reflection of something I remind you of in yourself, my color, hair, style of dress, the way I walk, talk, tap my feet, could be anything you see to evoke something in you to like or something you'd rather not see in me.

What do you see in the sunset out west of colors to dazzle, is it the beauty of creation, the presence of the moment or the view of your mind's eye when long ago and far away you proposed to her and she said yes.

Or, what of the child running barefoot through the grass, is it the playful innocence you see or yourself there in the arms and feet of play, your inner child wishing it could be free again.

And what of the plane that flies or the boat that sails, is it the shape, noise, wind or water you observe, or is it your adventurous spirit at the controls to guide the plane through the air or the boat across the sea.

And what of love in its many forms you find, flames of passion, tender embrace of affection, love lost or found, love of mankind, even the country you love you see in yourself.

Then there in the homeless, the dirty clothes, tangled hair, grocery sacks of despair, is it their sadness you see or but for circumstances, yourself in their plight.

So then the question begs to be asked, is it not what you see where you look but of what in yourself you see looking back.

Walking Boys

The day we took a walk you called us "Walking Boys," a cool breeze tickled our faces, adventure at every turn, stones to collect, puddles to splash, leaves to chase.

The people you met you said "Hello" to and wouldn't let it go until they said "Hello" back.

We raced across the park, you got a head start and won of course, you always did.

We played in the grass, planted a seed, "Will it grow, grandpa," you asked, "We'll see," I said, maybe in the spring if we check back.

"Let's get lost," you chuckled, no one will find us then, "Why not," I wondered and you said, "You know grandpa, we're Walking Boys."

Behind the Mask

Who am I, I must ask, the man behind the mask or is it masks to be worn, more than one to cover the truth, protect the darkness within.

What secrets must I keep hidden from the light, fearful of heaven and earth to crumble if the mask or masks be undone.

The truth of me I seek, once my guide, highest self, truth I despaired of knowing again, from what fears does the mask or masks hide of loss, separation from love's light.

Which way does the mask or masks face, surely the world my appearance can see from the side looking out, but what of the side I'm forced to see, my fears looking back at me.

The Ways of Love

What is it I want today, is it money I desire or maybe less doubt, fear or more faith I can have if I pray not in supplication but in affirmation of my divine right.

What should it be, anything that's good for me or others I may see in the course of life today, but I believe it will be love I choose as it's all that's ever needed anyway.

Yes, love is mine to express no matter what I do, where I go or who I meet, to say from the heart so sweet, "I love you."

I believe today I'll remind myself when in doubt to look within where love is rooted, the seed of creation once planted, the harvest plentiful to share.

I believe today I'll remind myself there's nothing to fear if I but let go of the reasons and let love's guidance and protection light the truth of my way, my intended destination.

I believe today I'll allow love's reminder of faith from the beginning implanted to trust the truth of myself and others on the path of spirit's guidance.

*I think today shopping for the week's sustenance,
I'll talk to all the strangers I can, smile and ask
them something about themselves they care to
share, and when checking out to be aware of the
cashier's workload, love's rays also to illumine
there.*

*I think today driving home I'll let a little love shine
on others going and coming my way that their day
is going well and if by chance someone cuts me
off, follows too close or weaves through traffic at
a fast pace, I'll direct a prayer of love their way for
heaven knows they surely need it.*

*And today I'll have more love to summon if I stop
for lunch and take a seat, the waitress slow to take
my order but apologetic, I'll find empathy to notice
she's overworked and stressed, a little love she'd
appreciate and be sure to tip her well before I go.*

*Let's see, where else today the ways of love to
express, sure to find plenty with family, friends,
neighbors, the trash truck driver, mailman, kids
coming and going from school and of course the
down hearted of life lost in one form or another, I'd
be blest to meet one or two of them.*

*So, today I've come to conclude there's really
no end to the ways of love's expression my
willingness to share.*

Mystery of Love

What can be said of love to speak of its truth as if the lofty mind would define what only the heart can know.

Words of love alone fail at meaning, even the sharpest tongues fail in its illusive task, the subject too deceptive to discern even for a rhyming bard's grasp.

One must look for love's mystery where it may be found, not in its sound so sweet, or in human exchange, but in the heart's deeper well from which to search beneath the labels of content, some loose and uncaring, others tightly wound and despairing, still others by rote vacuous of meaning.

It is only there in plain sight layers of deception peeled away, the truth of love forever remains for us to see.

Jewelry Man

*The Jewelry Man I happened to meet a sunny
morning in September, short man with a baseball
cap, blue jeans and Tee-shirt, smile to match the
sun's rays above his head.*

*Met his friend too as they were talking, sharing
their company at a far-off place, New Mexico's Ojo
Caliente its name.*

*I turned a corner, never knew what I'd find, place
of mystery, place of peace, place of sacred waters
flowing freely down a mountain side.*

*I got to talking as I always do, to discover the
who's, what's and where's of them, faces of
humanity to share, my new friends I visited there.*

*The Jewelry Man and his friend, teacher of the
young at a nearby school, revealed many things
that morning about life in and outside of them,
blessings of the day lived, friendship and the work
in New Mexico they did.*

*The teacher took his leave, the Jewelry Man
remained to display his craft for others to buy,
unpacking bags he had brought of rings for the
fingers and ears too, necklaces, broaches and
more, baubles and beads spread along a long table
for all to see who happened by.*

*As he worked, he talked of family, smiles to explain
love of wife, parents, grandkids too, and not to
forget the 3 p.m. football game he'd need to be to
see the grandkids play.*

*But for the moment he was at ease explaining his
craft of which he was pleased of the stones he'd
long gathered, Turquoise and more from his native
land.*

*The Jewelry Man, the label seems a misnomer
only to speak of part of him, his fare of rich colors
displayed, but so much more to be said of the
gentle spirit within I'd come that sunny morning in
September to know and appreciate.*

Blue Eyes

Blue eyes, dearest you've been given, could have been I suppose brown, green or even gray, if the creator was having a bad day.

But he was at his best when he came to you, your eyes he envisioned with thoughts of the oceans and skies so blue, he'd implant the same colors in you.

And then he sat back a bit and surveyed his work and decided he had more to do to define a special shade like no other just for you.

And so he searched the kingdom far and wide and little did he find to suit the task, must be other measures suitable he decided to locate the perfect shade of blue just for you.

The creator thought for a while and knew just what to do, he'd summon the palette, the large one only he could use of infinite colors to mix, he'd paint a color of blue just for you.

He went to work, took a while to get it just right for not any blue would do, but only one of a kind in all creation he'd choose just for you.

And when he took a dab of this, a dab of that and a few more dabs he knew it just right, then sat back having done his best, admired his work and called together all the kingdom to approve the perfection of your eyes so beautiful he'd created just for you.

Love Is

Love is tender, the spring leaf, the new wine, joy shared.

Love is burning, the summer passion, hearts entwined.

Love is fading, the fall leaves changing, lightly clinging.

Love is old, the barren winter, its time nearly passed.

Spiritual Journey

Of what is this spiritual journey you speak, journey of cosmic proportion, realm of divinity to seek.

Of what is your destination, from where have you begun and where will you be when you arrive where you're going and what will you see.

Of what is the truth of yourself you seek, the reason the soul must surely provide of spirit's guidance you're willing to follow.

And are you walking to or from yourself, such questions must be asked as each step you leave behind on the path the darkness for the light you wish to find.

Do you wrap yourself now in spirituality's blanket to warm the cold of past transgressions hidden in the folds of your false self from back when you had no control of where you were or where you began.

Do you travel light void of burdens, the baggage of unworthiness, doubt and uncertainty traded for faith and trust and sureness of the direction to be led.

And what if you stumble as you might, will you retreat to safety of the known, turn back from the divine light in fear as others have done when the truth becomes too elusive or hard to bear.

*So, of this journey you've chosen, or did it choose
you, what can you say except you've come far
enough to know there is the truth of you waiting
within your soul, where its always been.*

Troubled Man

He stood six two, two ten he liked to brag, towering over my six-year-old frame, this man my father, troubled man.

He wore manliness on his sleeve to hide unworthiness within, the mask thick and unrelenting from his demons to shield the truth of him, this man my father, troubled man.

He wrestled with life not knowing from where he came or was going, only the madness he'd never dispel, salvation's gifts deprived of him, this man my father, troubled man

He drank and womanized, escapes of delusion, purchase of brief happiness by a mind he didn't understand, unknowing self he thought he was and should have been, this man my father, troubled man.

He modeled for me a life created from the ragged fabric of his being, shaping and molding the clay, potter of the man he thought I should be, but never would or could be, this man my father, troubled man.

The manic-depressive diagnosis came much later, too late to end his suffering before Lithium could have helped him, this man my father, troubled man.

Life moved on, I'd discover the truth out from under him, but his truth forever to elude him until his last breath, this man my father, troubled man.

"Life is a mirror and will reflect back to the thinker what he thinks into it,"
Ernest Holmes

For Fear She'd Say Yes

The day I was so lonesome I asked her out, but hoped she'd say no for fear she'd say yes.

My stomach, butterflies floated the day I was so lonesome I asked her out, but hoped she'd say no for fear she'd say yes.

My mouth dryer than the Sahara, words hesitant on my lips the day I was so lonesome I asked her out, but hoped she'd say no for fear she'd say yes.

My words I worried I'd stutter the day I was so lonesome I asked her out, but hoped she'd say no, for fear she'd say yes.

My heart pounded in my chest the day I was so lonesome I asked her out, but hoped she'd say no for fear she'd say yes.

Awakening

Many months ago the other day I awoke from sleep, a dream I wished I'd never had of past transgressions against my truth, surely I could never recover so dark the sorrow so long I'd known of joy stolen from me of who I am.

Then day followed night and spirit said enough my child you've been too long in the shadows not knowing where to look, a better idea I have in mind just down the street and around the corner you'll fi nd New Dawn Center for Spiritual Living, a place not with one but many doors to open.

And so, I took spirit's advice and dressed my old self as best I could in the unworthy hand-me-downs from the past, carefully choosing just the right mask of fear to shut me in and keep others out.

Weeks came and weeks went, old self made the effort to fi t in and absorb the joy expressed on the faces and hearts of all who had been waiting there for me all those years.

I began to change as spirit intended so gradual I hardly noticed, but not easy of course or in a straight line and when I'd lapse in fear, doubt and confusion, there was always another further along the spiritual path to take my hand and guide my mind.

*Months went by, old self fought against the light
not about to relinquish command, my partner
for much too long, fear of what in the halls of my
new home, the hugs, the smiles, the music, the
messages and prayers, of myself I'd fi nd.*

*Old self and I wrestled more than once, the truth of
me stronger with each match, if not to win at least
no longer to forfeit in its grasp to settle for who I'd
been, but accept the truth of myself, the universe to
provide what I was willing to accept.*

Louise

*She stands five feet two, hands on her hips,
business on her lips to call in her kids, who'd best
scurry if it's supper they want before they go to
bed, She's Louise.*

*Tender as a twig and tough as an oak, love in her
eyes, demeanor steady as she goes, She's Louise.*

*Gone now, kids grown, life moved on but a safe bet
to say if there are little angels where she's at, five
feet two, hands on her hips, business on her lips,
when called in they'd best scurry if it's supper they
want before they go to bed, She's Louise.*

Moab Motorcycle Man

*A hot day, a scenic drive, somewhere north of
Moab we'd arrived, a stop beside the road, picture
to be taken.*

*He'd stopped the motorcycle opposite where I
crossed the road to the perfect picture place.*

*The lady on the back loosened her grip around his
waist, shook her hair loose from a helmet, smiled
as I said, "Hello."*

*He swung his long leg off, black boot jamming the
ground and stretched.*

*The man bigger and taller than most, wore tattered
jeans, old leather jacket, cracked and creased
from miles of motorcycle racket, a smile as
wide as the canyon behind us, a gentle giant he
seemed.*

*I said, "Hello," he didn't respond, said it again
and he pointed to his ears, road noise must
have deafened him, helmet would have helped I
believed.*

I tried the lady, saw her "Signing" him.

*He stood straight and smiled, thrust out a big
hand, a mighty grip I'd feel for a while, disheveled,
grimy from the road, yet smiling with his chosen
load, a John the Baptist wandering toward the
Christ, sack of Locusts on his back.*

*He had the Biblical beard, long and grey, something
about him, about the way he looked and looked
at me, a child I thought who never grew up who
seemed to say, "Nothing can stop me or stand in
my way."*

*We exchanged the usual, where from, where going
and where been, said he'd rode all the way from
Cleveland, showed me the Ohio plate on the back,
a big laugh to illustrate.*

*Let me shake your hand again he said as we
parted, a mighty grip I'd feel for a while.*

*Back across the road I watched them go, he revved
the bike, her grip tight around him once again, a
quick look for traffic, then away down the road from
where our moment together had been, me and the
Moab Motorcycle Man.*

*All that way without ears to hear, no little feat, but
then I suspect he heard a different beat, the voice
of faith within.*

The Man

Divine man, earthy, powerful, mighty, teacher man

Souls' man, potter, shaper, builder, healer man

Betrayed man, mocked, beaten, crucified man

Son of man, love, peace, joy, faith, spirit man

My man, her man, his man, their man, our man

Fall from Grace

*My troubled soul, wandering self of human
expression fighting to control so far from its
beginning, lost in the dark forest of confusion, fear
the handmaiden of unknowing answers of what had
happened to me.*

*The beginning of the end to begin again arrived
so suddenly as if ordained from cosmic origin, the
thread to unravel on the specific date and time to
explode as a failed star would collapse unto itself.*

*It was not I who was intended to be upon the
altar of earthly life to worship, sudden riches
so unworthy only to fold in retreat set by an
inconsequential event of the celestial seed planted
for the moment of my demise.*

*And so it was it came about without notice the
curtain split, the tender heart broken, separated
from divine source, needing protection when
none would come, the time the light went out and
darkness lit.*

*In fury, I punched the wall, anger unleashed again
and again until it failed to yield no more; spent,
I fell to my knees to lie in the pool of tears I'd
created.*

Well intended were those who would step in harm's way of my torrent, bless them for their efforts to ease my pain and comfort as well their confused state as I lay in agony wanting only to escape short of death from misery.

The flood of tears in due time would wash enough anguish from my chest to again breathe the breath of my heart's desire, two lovely arms around me held for all time my pain to her breast.

Bakugans

*Be careful where you step my friend you must
know why, Bakugans are everywhere down here
and up in the sky.*

*Bakugans are all about, high up, down low, in the
middle or in the corner, I think I see one hiding over
there somewhere.*

*Bakugans are watching, at home in their shells,
big, little, nice or scary, some are skinny, some are
hairy, some quite contrary.*

*So, best be wise my friend and be alert if from their
shells they suddenly spurt you'd best be ready,
cause Bakugans are everywhere.*

Madness

*Madness, from where do you spring, origin of the
fire of haunted being burning of other fires to light.*

*Fear, is madness your port of terror, storms on the
ocean of your mind with no preserver to keep you
afloat.*

*Doubt from whence of the universe do you burn
bright, maddening confusion of uncertain darkness
to search the secure stars that have eluded you.*

*Hate, most maddening of all, do you wonder
what had happened on your sprit's path for your
shattered soul to seek such retribution.*

*Heart, even of love's design, is wont to madness
driven if unrequited finds its demons of memory so
sad of love to have gone bad.*

*Madness, ask of origin and carefully choose the
answer not to be found in fear, doubt, hate, heart,
or love, but in your escape or your surrender.*

Long Legged Man

From out of my movie seat I tried to make the stairs from the row I'd have to navigate to find relief for gathering urgency, a very long-legged man I'd have to negotiate.

"Excuse me Sir," I'm in dire straights needing to urinate, if you'd but stand and let me by, never to know why he failed to heed my plea, the narrowest of expanse to navigate between his knees and the back of the seat ahead of him.

A bit wobbly I must say, balance being my affliction, I began to struggle back and forth in the narrow passageway to find a hold atop the seatback ahead of him, only to startle the occupant, "Excuse me," I replied to mumbling discontent.

"Watch my purse," I heard it said as I wobbled by the lady beside the long-legged man, I wobbled one way and then the other, grasping her seatback, much to her chagrin, better than to have fallen in her lap.

The lady said, "Ouch," "Excuse me," I said, sorry I'd caused pain, but no choice in the matter, my path unbearably narrow by the long-legged man who refused to stand for my departure.

Then at last I gained a step beyond the lady and the long-legged man, but still to negotiate two ladies between me and the stairs, staring as if to say, "Who is this crazy man."

Finally I found the railing to guide me down the steps I sought, free at last I reasoned, the relief I sought now in sight; but, given all the fuss and rants and apologies, I had to ask, would it have not been better to stay put in my seat and peed my pants.

Tears of Tenderness

*Tears of the tender heart impress, sweet nectar
of soul expressed of the heart to bleed of love
and joy of life's humanness.*

*Tears of the tender heart impress, the child's
smile demands, the joyful soul evokes love's
tender flow.*

*Tears of the tender heart impress, emotions
stirring, release of spirit's oneness with other
hearts' loveliness, light within glowing, wisdom's
knowing in love's tender flow.*

*Tears of the tender heart impress, beckoned forth
to flow, knowing of other lives' faces, hearts lost
in separation from spirit's wholeness, light within
burning dim, that once burned bright, tears to bleed
for their plight.*

No Stars at Night

Daddy, why are there no stars at night, shining bright like I know they should, question innocent enough to ask if unseen she believed they must not be.

No stars at night heaven gone to sleep, I'd never understand, couldn't be right, no stars at night zillions of miles from earth's grasp to twinkle bright all night long, a little ones' longing to see the stars of night.

No stars at night could it be God playing tricks on you and me, their brilliance kept from us and this little girl at my knee to see.

No stars at night, they were there as a boy who in the darkness on the warm grass of a summer's night could see more stars than grains of sand in all the oceans shores, to reach out to grab a few in the palm of my hand.

No stars at night, it's a pity for man to have built city lights to block them from view even on the darkest of nights.

No stars at night, what must I say to ease her fears they've gone away, best not to speak of man's intervention in their disappearance for she wouldn't understand, but instead to have her know like God's spirit ever present, the stars are there, have been and always will be, to be seen not with eyes in darkness looking up, but with hearts in light looking within.

God's Street

Street of hope's shadow, hunger, homelessness, asphalt ribbon of bars, pawn shops, cheap motels, tattoo parlors, life's scars.

Street of nations, wanderers, cart pushers, panhandlers, alley drunks, easy drugs, rag clothes, broken dreams and street preachers.

Mean street, hard life street, dead-end street, God's street, my street.

God has swept away the past
we keep looking for.

The First Time

The first time we made love was the last, the end of innocence and curious wonderings of what such union was all about beyond the vulgar word to describe the mechanics of it.

The first time we made love, if you can call it that, was where other first times were consummated, in the dark of moonlight in the wooded area off the country road, a mile from town in the back seat of my old Chevy.

The first time we made love, if you can call it that, to describe the awkward fumbling of teenage expression void of romantic feeling lost in youthful passion, wondering if we were doing it right.

The first time we made love it hurt you; and, I felt your pain and wanted to stop, but you urged me to complete the act to at least be recorded as the first time event, we could say experienced we were and let it go at that.

The first time we made love was the last as I moved away not long thereafter and there would never be another time to know each other like that in the dark of moonlight in the wooded area off the country road, a mile from town in the back seat of my old Chevy.

The Greatest Grandson

To the Greatest Grandson in the whole universe,

I think this book (Don't Sweat the Small Stuff) may help you navigate some of the whirlpools and eddies of teenage life. I know these years can be difficult, fraught with figuring out who you are and where you fit in with the grand scheme of things, suddenly different and perplexing.

I know firsthand, okay so it was sixty-five years ago, when I was suddenly thrust between the days of dependent childhood into the cauldron of changes of body and mind, challenges of discovery, questioning, and impatience of answers to find.

Suddenly there are pressures of conformity, expectations of others, peers and those closest to you, directions which can be at odds with your moral compass.

It's at these times when the most significant question you or anyone can ask themselves and continue asking throughout their lives, is "Who Am I?"

The answer becomes obscured in the noise of competing voices, but the special person you are, the innate character you possess, your sense of love and care of others, more important than the labels of achievement, will serve you well in these years and beyond and when difficulties arise, and they will, answers will come not from others but from within yourself.

Love always,
The Greatest Grandpa in the whole universe

Veil of Distortion

Quick, my friend look close and see spirit's light of all that is and all that may be, promise of faith, trust, freedom divine, the blessed place within to rest.

Look, be quick to see all before the veil of distortion would fall, to see the whole, feel its presence, hear its joy, the voice of discovery of the oneness you seek, before it all disappears so suddenly.

Quick, if only for a moment you linger in the divine's grasp, free of doubt and fear, before you must question what had briefly been there to give you peace.

Be quick to discover new ideas found within the light of journey's day, before distortion of night sets in to surely stay.

Oh, you must wonder of the cruelty the veil imposes in sudden absence from joyful musing, separation from glory once glimpsed to fear it may never appear again.

Be sure my friend the joy you've seen shines bright behind the veil, distortion ever thinned by the truth of being's light, one day completely rent never to hide the darkness again.

Devil's Handmaidens

The Devil's handmaidens Fear and Doubt deigned to still the light of life's joy, pain of distortion to implant.

Fear and Doubt have you no shame, evil providers your work to do to hide the light of truth in darkness wrapped.

If but more faith to summon from fear's grasp, more trust from doubt's clasp, then surely to say fear no longer to dwell in me, doubt be gone from heart's place unwelcome there.

Fear and Doubt, duet of darkness, purveyors of separation to roil the waters of life's demands, mere veils of love's face to mask.

Fear unfounded, Doubt unclaimed may be known if each day prevails, a little more faith, a little more trust, a little more willingness to know only love.

Window Washer

A slight man, talked a lot, bit nervous too, fidgety when he moved, not sure where to land.

Met him at a bus stop many years ago, seemed friendly enough to pass the day, we talked the wait away.

Curious I was about what he carried, his tools he said, a bucket and long handled squeegee.

A window washer he was plain to see but traveled light didn't have a car, didn't need one, he said.

A traveling window washer he was with customers all over town, prices were right with his overhead.

Our ride together was short but before I left he revealed once a big truck he had with ladders, a Ford no less, bright red too, a sign attached to advertise his work.

Been washing windows forever he said, houses, office buildings, churches, restaurants, even a school or two.

Hard times came along, as hard times do, forced to sell the truck, bright red, a sign attached, ladders too.

He paused a moment to reflect to make sure I knew it was okay with him making do.

A time or two thereafter, I'd be driving by, and there he'd be waiting for the bus, the window washer, his bucket, long handled squeegee and his pride too.

Love Is

*Love is tender, the spring leaf, the new wine,
heartstrings to play upon time.*

*Love is burning, passion of two hearts entwined in
harmony as one.*

*Love is strong, solid oak root of life's longing
deeply embedded in life.*

Calling the Cows

*Remember the day you pulled off the country road,
walked over to the fence to call the cows, see if
they'd come over to where you stood.*

*They were way off in the field chewing grass
ignoring the man at the fence calling them to come
to him.*

*You cupped your hands around your mouth and
began to bellow in your finest bass voice, sounded
like a bull, maybe a little more mellow.*

*The old gals perked up their ears, tails a twitching,
"Let's go girls, old bull's a itching for romance."*

*They came a running in twos and threes, udders a
swinging, heading for the trees where you stood by
the fence.*

*They were in a hurry it was plain to see but stopped
suddenly in confusion of only you at the fence
bellowing at them.*

*They huddled together heads turning hoping to
see the object of their yearning, but with no bull in
sight, turned tails and went back way off in the field
where they had been before you called them in.*

Divine Inspiration

*Oh God eternal, do you mean to express yourself
through me in the words I write for others to know
the wonders of your divinity.*

*Do you inspire every word that comes to me to tell
of the joy of life, the people the places the triumphs
the defeats that bind together mankind's place in
your infinite creation.*

*Do you take my hand when I sit down to write, my
fingers to find the right keys to form the story of
spirit's love for all that is, was, and ever will be.*

*Do you use the gift you've given me to express
your love of humanity, a purpose you made for me
to see divinity within each of us here on the earthly
plane.*

*And when I write of the child, the smile of an angel
to light the darkness, is it your hand expressing
your wishes of the way the words I would form.*

*You must know now of what I write and be pleased
in each verse implanted in me of you and your
creation of the universe for all to see.*

Uncommon Words

Toilet Water, Trash Can, Receptacle Bin, useful words to most of us but to the poet words of action to roll delicately off the tongue, toilet water gently, trash can a bit harsh, receptacle bin lively in the dance of verse.

The words of use only terms of function for the common man his employ of necessity's needs, but to the wordsmith of verse the gracious dance of mastered language, toilet water fl owing gracefully across the mind, trash can a slice of subtlety, receptacle bin itself somewhat a rhyme.

Mere words of course more or less labels quickly dismissed but to the bard's trade the stuff of which poetry is made.

Thirty-Three-Thousand Feet

One morning about ten I scanned the skies from my window seat at thirty-three-thousand feet.

An hour before we'd taken off a winter storm cleared enough space our pilot's visual bearings to discern, between the runway below and the dark cloud bank above.

Our moment between day and night didn't last for long, just a few minutes until the dark cloud enveloped us for good in its grasp we were committed.

The pilot his eyes to scan the instruments of attitude, speed and turn and bank, back and forth up and down to keep us upright in our climb to the altitude assigned.

It seemed we'd climbed forever that morning through clouds dark and foreboding I could see from my window seat.

But then suddenly it appeared, just a glimmer of expectation the sun chose to reveal at the top of my window seat, teasing with something more glorious of morning to come.

The next moment of wonder the nose of the airliner
breaking the plane of the flat bank of darkness
to behold the brightest of light the sun's glory
beaming off the white clouds shining at flight level
thirty-three-thousand feet.

Now, some would fail to see significance of what
transpired by which we'd flown through darkness
to suddenly break into God's light waiting there, his
magnificence to share at thirty-three-thousand feet.

In Ages Place

Today the end of yesterday's embrace, entwined anew in ages place.

Today to celebrate sunrises and sunsets of days in ages place.

Today to drink deeply of love and grace forever in ages place.

Tomorrow to reflect of all that's been of love and life in ages place.

Who Am I

Who am I, dare I ask of what I may find to question of myself who I've become from where I began.

Am I the one with the bag of labels accumulated off the shelf of the world's library, each a façade of the real me from birth to death.

Or am I the many masks I've worn to hide within and shut the world out, separation a toxic tonic of protection from the truth left far behind.

May I dare ask if I've become the role I played of the script of life written for me by others who thought they knew best of who I was and should become, an extension of the scripts they were assigned to play.

And what of the script of the divine writer who fashioned me in spirit's image to be of love, power and wholeness of the universe to know all there is and all there ever could be.

If I were to climb a mountain to find the truth of myself waiting there for me, would I recognize its nature so different perched on the rock of eternity for the day when I'd dare to sit there and ask, "Who Am I?"

And if I should never ask for fear of knowing, never question who I've become and continue to sleep through the only life I've known, how sad it may be the small voice planted within the seed of divinity from which I began, forever drowned in life's stormy seas.

"…no mistaken sense of self should keep us from the pleasure of knowing who we are,"
Rev. Dr. Margaret Stortz

Barnstormer

*His cockpit open, face shielded from the wind,
hands on the stick, feet on the rudders banking and
turning searching for a barn roof with the name of a
town on it.*

*He's a barnstormer, one of a daring few flying noisy
oil burning airplanes to take others aloft, make a
buck or two.*

*He scouts the field below, this barnstormer man,
no ruts or rocks to ruin a landing, scare everyone
including him.*

*He turns to town to buzz the streets flying low to
let the people know to come and take a ride in the
airplane he flies this day, leaflets he drops to show
the way and for the cost of a few bucks they can
fly in the open cockpit airplane for everyone to see
how brave they are to go up with the barnstormer
man.*

*Boys and girls strain to see the flying man looping
above rocking his wings, showing off his skills in
his noisy flying machine.*

*They come in jalopies, bicycles too, some walk,
others run to be first in line for an airplane ride.*

"Step right up little lady, big man you there with the girlfriend, only three bucks," he goes to work in the morning sun, "fly you right over town to wave at your friends, thrill of a lifetime, safe as all get out."

Young men, old men, wives and kids arrive, a few grannies in the crowd, some excited and willing, some scared and hesitant of airplanes falling from the sky.

The rides go on all during the day, the screaming, yelling and acting brave, tales to savor and tell of flying up, flying down, flying over the little town until flying with the barnstormer ends for the day.

As the sun sets in the west, the crowd disperses, flight time to write upon their logs of life, stories to tell for generations of the day the barnstormer came to town and up and away with him they went.

As for the barnstormer, he counts the dollar bills not a lot, but feels rich of his delight to fly the skies in search of those grounded to share a little flight time with.

So now in the cockpit the engine running, he dons his goggles, releases the brakes and flies off into the sunset another barn to find with the name of a town to buzz, more men, women, kids and a few grannies there to go flying with him.

Ojo Caliente

*Ojo Caliente, spent a week there one day at the end
of a journey through the history of healing mineral
waters flowing through centuries of enchanted
land.*

*Waters beloved and blessed by ancient Indian
tribes on their march through sacred lands a
step ahead of the white man's reign of terror and
domination.*

*The healing waters tell a story of ages before
civilization of northern New Mexico, waters of
extreme heat, summoned by man-made pools, now
mineral springs of pleasure for modern day natives
and visitors who gather there.*

*Ojo Caliente, spent a week there one day yearning
for more, but thankful for the native Indians so
long ago, expecting another mountain to trespass,
discovered a fountain of youth to bless.*

Soar Little Bird

Soar little bird, high above earthly bonds, flap your wings, harder still.

Soar little bird, test your flight, up even more where the big eagles fly.

Soar little bird up and up, up where the air is thin, higher than before, all the way up to heaven's door.

To Dream

To dream of life's wonders, life's delights, life's mysteries, blessed days and blessed nights.

To dream of life's gifts, places far away, mountains, animals, rivers to play.

To dream of life's happiness, gifts given, gifts to give, all things of love to have.

To dream of life's freedom, what is within and what is without of life to dream about.

The Bus Lady

She got off the bus that day I was walking her way,
short lady, bit stooped with her load, big suitcase
on wheels, a bag on her shoulder.

She walked my way from the bus stop across the
street taking her time for the light to turn green, our
paths to cross in the neighborhood from which I
was leaving and she was coming.

I said, "Hello there" and she stopped for a spell, her
name I asked, she didn't respond, so I asked again
a little louder and she pointed to her hearing aids in
derision, the batteries dead.

I raised my voice and got her attention, noticed the
Jesus Cross around her neck and her age told me
she'd been a bit bent even without her load to tote
from the bus she rode to get where we were at.

She lingered long enough for me to know she
didn't live in the neighborhood but once a week
came to spend awhile with a lady in need of her
care, a few streets south and around the corner.

We talked some more, said she didn't have family
nearby and spent her days looking after others
around town near a bus stop she'd need, her only
mode of transportation you see.

I offered to carry her bags to the destination but she'd have none of that, so I wished her well and she returned the favor, blessing me before we parted.

Not much more for me to say about the lady I met that day other than life not of great riches but of gratitude for the journey, a bus to ride, burdens to bear for someone else in need of her care.

I Hardly Knew You

My mother dear you gave me life it's true, but after that I hardly knew you.

The first few years of your embrace, the nurturing love of your grace, but after that I hardly knew you.

I sat upon your lap, your gentle arms around me reading a story, but after that I hardly knew you.

I was six when events transpired the marriage of which I came dissolved, and after that I hardly knew you.

The years went by and there may have been a phone call or two, questions to go unanswered by those who kept me from you, but after that I hardly knew you.

I got older and on my own, you'd moved on, remarried, another son to raise, I saw you a few times but too much had elapsed of hearts broken to resume a mother-son relationship.

And now many years later you're gone and I'm long removed from the day you gave me birth, thoughts of you dimmed, darkness to hide all of what might have been.

That's about all there is to say about loss so long ago, but I'm grateful for those first six years, because after that I hardly knew you.

Mom and Dad

Bruised knee, tears come, hurts a lot, please stop, mom's embrace, tender words, tears dry, better now.

Mom knows best.

Star Wars fantasies, bad guys to fight before bed, just a little more time, please dad.

Sleepy eyes, firm words now, off to bed my son, different tears flow at the way things have gone.

Dad knows best.

Life Without Music

Life without music I can't imagine, airwaves void of magical sweetness woven by the master's touch to bring smiles from the heart in life's drudgery to escape.

Had God left music out of the eternal plan certainly not on purpose as would seem against nature, vibrations of heavenly harmony would not for the soul to ever hear.

If the ear were to open only to the spoken word having never heard angelic expression, choirs of heaven and earth singing would all have been for naught.

Life without music, no radios to play or through the air waft to the ear another way the gentle or harsh melodies soft or loud even offensive to some tastes, but always there to be heard if by choice the listener makes.

No music, what would it mean life devoid of emotions tickled, teased and inflated by an artist's creation so intended but never to be realized only prevented, the artist as well never to have been.

*No music of life, too unreal to imagine we'd
been deprived of to make our way having never
heard the voices soft or loud, shrill or silly, the
instruments play, the child's little tune of nursery
rhyme, the opera majestic, the choir of sopranos,
altos, tenors, and bass, the lover's croon, the
showman's exuberant sounds of storytelling, even
singing in the shower would never have been.*

*So we say in our elation, having realized the world
without music would have been a much different
place, are happy to know the creator divine
intended all along music to be a part of the eternal
plan.*

What If

*I had a thought today a bit wild I must say some
would say crazy but what do they know the
wonders of life to play with if you'd dare a little
crazy to be aloft in a tree doesn't make sense but
rhymes no less a little crazy indeed this thought
of mine but no less meaningful to me.*

*I had a thought today and here it goes to toss
around throw in the air bounce on the ground talk
of it with a clown shake it out hoist it up the flag
pole you get the idea shake it from convention's
grasp if for once or for many times before life's
last dance the breath assured to murmur I had
some fun was outrageous and crazy in absurdity.*

*So if you've gotten this far with this crazy verse
and scratching your head or worse of what
you've heard take heed my friend you're not
alone you see all life can be crazy if you let it
be and only ask "What if" before taking the last
breath.*

*What if I'd caught raindrops in my mouth let a jar
of grasshoppers loose in a friend's car brought
lightening bugs in the house to glow in the dark?*

*What if I'd played golf and not kept score or missed
a putt intentionally when the score was tied flew
through a cloud upside down taken a shower
with my clothes on rode a bike backwards gone
downtown instead of uptown?*

*What if I'd praised a performance when it stunk
panned one when it was great laughed at a joke that
wasn't funny went late to church and sat in the front
row opened more doors for pretty girls and homely
ones too stopped to tie someone else's shoe.*

*What if I'd had more second helpings third ones
too listened more and talked less petted more
handsome dogs ugly ones too smiled at more
pretty girls homely ones too?*

*What if I had learned a new language flew a plane
sailed a boat zipped across a canyon on a wire got
up early to see a sunrise stayed up late to see the
stars asked the prettiest girl for a date and kissed
her too?*

*What if I left my umbrella home when it rained
started a conversation with a stranger cried with
someone hurting cried in church let others be right
more than wrong.*

*What if I saw another person behind their mask and
from behind mine been outrageous made a fool of
myself gone to a movie late and couldn't find a seat?*

*What if I slept late when I wanted to get up early got
up early when I wanted to sleep late ran out of gas
just for the hell of it smelled more than one flower
in a bouquet?*

*What if I raced my grandson and let him win
pushed someone across the finish line ahead of
me actually enjoyed waiting walked through a mud
puddle in my best shoes read a book and never
remembered a word of it?*

*What if I let the dog sleep in the bed between the
sheets smiled at someone in the car next to me
bought a stranger a meal anonymously brought
another home for dinner just to eat?*

*What if I'd been more generous with my treasures
given more of my time and talents played dumb
when the kids thought they were pulling one over
on me gone to a game and sat in the top row ran a
race and finished last?*

*What if I had spilled soup on my best shirt left my
comb home on a windy day brushed my teeth with
the other hand milked a cow drove a tractor slept in
a barn made love in a hayloft?*

*What if I had eaten more ice cream helped more
bums fed the homeless lost my car keys in the
refrigerator lost my car in the parking lot skipped a
haircut or walked upstairs backwards?*

*What if I had climbed a mountain rafted a stream
fished in a river without any bait walked through a
puddle in my bare feet wrote a poem and left all the
commas out?*

*What of these things to do many I have managed
but many remain before my last breath to ask
"What if" these things I had done?*

Hey Buddy

"Hey Buddy, how's it going," "How you doing Young Lady, having a good day?" I'm known to say quite often to everyone I meet, just being friendly I suppose, but find I really care about the Buddies and Young Ladies over Fifty I meet and the day together we are blessed to share.

A day at the grocery I most enjoy with fellow veterans hands to shake and a "Thank you for your service," a minute to take to get the particulars, and when passing or approaching a Buddy or Young Lady over Fifty, just can't help myself to stop and exchange a word or two with them.

But then when I'm tardy to help my dear wife put the groceries in the car, she has to ask, "Do you have to talk to everyone in the store." "Yes I do Young Lady over Fifty," and by the way, "How's your day going, dear?"

The Day Dad Sold My Car

The day many years ago now lost in the forgiveness that enveloped and healed all that was and had come before, a lesson to teach of life's indiscretion of human interaction in the vast sea of reflection of transgressions of what a father might be and do to a son.

A minor thing when held to the light of today's introspection, no less the pain of then the day dad sold my car.

The car like the sweetness, if I may be sentimental, of first love, I'd entrusted it to his care while away at sea but should have known the log of trust of our relationship was barren of history between us as we'd gone along.

My car, she was a beauty, '47 Ford blue, customized too, so sleek, her V8 really purred over the many years and trips we'd take when I was seventeen, never faltering I took good care of her and she never failed me.

Not long after returning to port and shore bound I'd be, I wanted my car on the base to go on liberty maybe even come home again one day to stay for good, drive my car across the USA.

*And so I called one morning from the phone booth
on base, my stepmother answered and her voice
faltered when I said I'd be there soon to get my car
to bring back with me.*

*"Your Dad sold it," what else could she say, the
words cut like a knife and I knew she was sad he'd
do such a thing, but not too surprising knowing his
devious ways of putting money in the bank.*

*And so it was and that was that, what more could I
do or say that day of events that transpired some
two thousand miles away, just best let it go and
know with time I'd have another car to call mine
and best keep it close at hand this time.*

A Slice of Life

This morning I set out a haircut to get a little late I was but did not fret, believing my hair cutting friend who had not yet arrived would soon be there to take care of me.

I settled in a cozy chair to fiddle with my device perusing affirmations of life I've discovered within myself of who I am when I'm authentic, waiting patiently for my hair cutting friend to walk through the door.

Many minutes passed as they do, the clock on the wall telling its story, my friend was much too late and I wondered if I should remain when it dawned on me you silly goose, you're here a day too early a haircut to get.

Oh My, I thought, now what should I make of this, wondered if I'd lost my marbles, blame it on lost sleep the night before, there must be a reason, a lesson in store, a possibility not thought of before.

And so I bid the ladies of the hair shop adieu, be back tomorrow same time I said, but not all is lost, you got to see me and I got to see you, I laughed, they laughed too.

*I quickly forgot my mental lapse and started for my
car when a thought beckoned of a store close by to
procure bagels for my wife to enjoy.*

*It was there I held the door for another being
emerging from her car, noting the pains of old age
getting up the steps where for her I waited, a smile
of gratitude on her lips for the railing and this man
holding the door for her.*

*Say, how do you like your Honda I asked as
I always do when I see one similar and she
brightened with reply she loved it and her husband
had one he loved too, the conversation continued.*

*So reliable we agreed and could have gone on all
day about the subject and maybe more of which we
were blessed, if not interrupted by bagels to buy,
the next great thing in our lives that day.*

*Then passing again on my way out, a brief visit as
she waited to give her order, I bathed momentarily
in her smile and heard her say, "Thank you sir,
you've made my day."*

*Not bad I had to think as she'd made my day too,
connection made with another on the spiritual path,
and couldn't help but wonder of what I'd of missed
had I not been remiss of my haircut day, the laughs
shared with those in the shop, bagels for my wife
to treat and best of all the lady with the Honda and
a fondness for bagels placed there for me to share
a slice of love of life with.*

*I have chosen to love and be loved and
that has made all the difference.*

Change

Change, a word of resistance, a word I rather not call a new place to live, comfortable in the old house on Status Quo Street.

Why so much opposition do I feel when something new comes along to disturb my reverie of what is, fear of what change might bring, what in this instance might happen.

How must I get from here to there to know change is good and natural of life to proceed, not to fear to seek of where the answers lie or in which direction I believe.

Shall I consult with the healers outside of myself to gain the way to power of decision, which they may impart should I seek.

No, I believe I must if I am to know all to be revealed of change invisible, discover the answers where they have always been, here in that place within.

New Dawn

New Dawn, what comes to mind; New Dawn, say it again, say it many times, New Dawn.

Sunrise I bet you conjure, morning reds and blues all too vivid, could be new beginning or beginnings you wish were true, could be anything the mind wills you, even new dollar bills if you're of a monetary bent, or anything else you might choose to make of it, anything you desire to appear.

A different view a higher mind proposes, vision beyond morning light, glimpse of heart's greatest delight, not far off to be sought or hidden from knowing to discover or uncover its meaning.

New Dawn, elusive it's been, but going within we find, not what's been searched for outside, but truth, new ideas, awareness of who we are and have always been, we awake to a New Dawn more glorious than a thousand previous ones, greater than a million new bills or anything outside of us we've imagined.

Dylan

*We had a dog, named him Dylan after the Welsh
poet, rightly so being Welsh, a Springer Spaniel of
noble birth to have a noble name.*

*He joined us as a puppy a few months old and
among the litter to view, he sat quietly and watched
never blinking an eye, his brothers and sisters all
over me competing for attention, I knew he was the
one I'd take home that day.*

*He grew by leaps and pounds and we bonded,
a family dog meant to be but really decided he
belonged to me.*

*I took him along most places I went and he loved
to ride his head out the window, ears flapping in
delight, tongue hanging to the side, barking at
every dog he'd see looking back at him and me.*

*Dylan shined when our grandson came along
and they romped on the floor, he consented to a
toddlers play, sometimes rough he never seemed
to care or yelp, content to just go along with the
pulls and yanks and rides on his back, as if to say,
"Hey, I was once a pup who liked to play rough."*

Dylan, a bird dog bred to hunt, but never trained as such, so was left to chase the squirrels and rabbits to harass, but don't believe one he ever caught, at least that we're aware of.

He'd pull on the leash when walked as if he couldn't wait to get along the path and be the first to arrive at the destination and the first to arrive back.

He'd fuss with other dogs aplenty and bark and scowl in resentment they dared to share his walking path when he was using it that particular time of day.

Time passed and he reached full growth, weighing fifty pounds he thought small enough to be held and cuddled every chance he'd get on my wife's lap.

Dylan was a fine dog, the best dog we'd ever had of a long line of pets, who loved to catch the door before it closed and spring through in a split second to roam the neighborhood and dare us to catch him.

He'd wait patiently on the patio when we grilled out for someone to vacate his seat and jump up to pounce on a burger he thought surely his, and didn't mind if it was rare, medium, or pink.

As Dylan got older he didn't like being left alone, wondering how we could do such a thing to a dog as fine as him, and after all, a member of the family.

*More years passed as they do and Dylan began
to slow down, older and gray, stiffer too, but still
made the effort to walk, his leash around his neck
connected.*

*He turned fifteen and a noticeable change came
over him, less enthused about his usual pleasures,
content to sleep the day away between his meals
and other endeavors.*

*Then the day came we dreaded to let him go the
saddest of all days we'd had with him, held him
close and thanked him for being part of our family
for so long and told him how much he was loved,
the drug administered, he peacefully slept, Dylan
the Welsh Springer Spaniel, the best dog we'd ever
had.*

Solo

The day we soloed the little airplane and me the first time alone with her and first time for her with me, the sun painting low rays across the runway connecting compass headings three sixty and one eight.

We'd been together for several months our love affair blossomed in her nature of stability and my tender mastery of her controls, the little airplane and me.

We'd been aloft many times that summer in the dance of nuance of our attraction, straight and level, banking turns, stalls, slow flight and cross-country excursions, but not yet alone, just the little airplane and me.

When landing I first tried she scolded me to be gentle and groaned in agony when I bounced her suddenly back into the air to try again to stay firmly planted, I'd come to learn if I'd treat her like a lady, she'd be nice to me.

"Think you're about ready," instructor said as we taxied out that evening June eighth, nineteen sixty-two, not a whiff of wind, the sock hung limp, sun settling even lower, a few touch and goes and we'd see, he grinned.

*The third time on final he called for a full stop, said
it was time to get out and leave her alone with me
and me with her, three touch and gos and don't
forget the carburetor heat, a common omission of
first timers like me.*

*So together many times we'd been, the first time
alone we flew, the runway rushing by, lifting off
at seventy the speed into the sun's rays across
the path we'd chosen for our first time, the little
airplane and me.*

*We reached five hundred on the altimeter and
turned crosswind as was the pattern to proceed,
downwind leg, base and final approach we flew, I
suddenly aware the only pilot was me to smile at
my good fortune to be at last alone with her, the
little airplane and me.*

Music Man

*He isn't tall in a measured sense but with music
he's above the rest behind a keyboard, elegant
in its own right, sets upon a little stand of his
choosing.*

*He plays the ivories to the listener's delight, hands
moving, feet tapping, really grooving, the music
man.*

*Soprano Sax in hand a look of profundity pleased
to play its high pitched brassy sound, he fingers
the openings only he knows are there, perfect
pitch, head bobbing in time, the music and the
music man.*

*He runs his hands over the board and back again,
takes up the horn, sure is busy, cheeks puffy,
blowing notes the cylinder delivers the horn
exhausts with special thunder the splendor of the
music man.*

*Keyboard again, he plays the ivories as one, smiles
a lot, laughs too, the horn, the keys, the notes, the
beat, the music man.*

The Writer

The real writer emerges, the one of word play, of images and creative description, of turning words to uncover deeper treasures, the depth attained at the writer's discretion and the reader's pleasure.

Old Thoughts

Old thoughts time to go, past time I'd say to fade away in truth's light.

Old thoughts time to go, no longer to dwell within, lingering so long there you've been.

Old thoughts time to go to let new thoughts, waiting in the wings to begin.

Old thoughts time to go back where you began so long ago never to return again.

Spirit Struggle

*Why struggle my friend with what spirit offers,
kingdom of glory to give the love and good of the
universe untold riches greater than gold, wonders
more than the planets, light more than the stars,
the kingdom not outside, above, or around to find,
but here within where its always been.*

*Why struggle when such blessings await, gifts
freely given without condition beloved for the
taking.*

*Why struggle from some dark place like Job of old
to wrestle divinity's gifts more powerful than your
denial.*

*Is faith you lack or doubt to harbor of the
abundance promised, love and peace taught,
wisdom to set the way clear.*

*Why struggle with truth coming across the waters
of life to be seen not in all outside of you, but at
home within.*

The Man I Met

*I met a man about fifty years ago at a place
long since passed, nevertheless kept alive by
remembrance of the halls of learning we'd gone
to find our life's meeting, maybe by chance, but I
know better than that.*

*A little older and wiser than others of the time
there to study for life ahead, he a man of numbers
to account of financial matters, me of the written
word to document life's stories, we met maybe by
chance, but I know better than that.*

*We worked hard to make the grade and learn
from those wise in numbers and the writing trade
preparing for success to come, the loves of our
lives joining our union in learning back then.*

*I moved away from the place of our meeting as
friends sometimes must do, he of deeper roots
stayed put where he'd been planted.*

*We thrived in our chosen vocations, children came
along, grandchildren too, as life moved from day
to day, year to year now fifty or more have passed
since we met maybe by chance, but I know better
than that.*

We stayed in touch through the years exchanging cards and letters, phone calls, and get togethers in neutral places where we shared old stories of the many memories we'd made from the company of friendship since we met, maybe by chance, but I know better than that.

And now those years have passed too quickly, we've turned old by life's standards, but stayed young by other measures, he now eighty, I not far behind, both bowed a bit by life's ills but not bent, this man I met maybe by chance, but I know better than that.

Who You Disrespect

You who would choose to sit or kneel when Glory passes by, the star-spangled song of honor playing, I would have you see it's not the flag you disrespect or even your country.

It's the young Marine who climbed Iwo Jima's mountain in '45, buddies falling right and left bloodied and broken machine gunned to death, never faltering, moving upward to take freedom from tyranny's grasp.

It's the bomber crew cold and scared over Europe's gray skies long ago dropping its load on Nazism's face who back to base never returned.

It's the sailors forever entombed in the Battleship Arizona at Pearl Harbor in the wake of '41s savage attack.

It's the foot soldier cold and worried in '44 slogging through the forests and hills of a foreign land, the Battle of the Bulge all hell breaking loose, bleeding and dying to break the enemy's back.

It's the modern-day warrior around the world leaving life and limb behind to keep terrorism's threat from your shores.

And so my friend wrapped in your cozy blanket of free speech and political pettiness, when you take a knee instead of standing like a man, refuse to doff your hat or turn a blind eye in protest when Glory passes by, remember it's not the Flag or your country you disrespect, it's the Marine, Airman, Sailor, Soldier who went to war for you and never came back.

Fear of Being Me

*Fear of being me, fear of being free, free of pains
of the past, free to ride in faith's carriage, free to let
go after a lifetime of doubt, free to soar on trust's
carpet of knowing and certainty, a glorious feeling
it is to be free.*

*I began to enjoy the present when
I stopped fearing the past.*

Awake to Possibility

What if I woke up when others were still asleep to see things differently, to see possibilities.

What if I could see within myself a greater glory than I've noticed looking outside, if only I woke up to its calling me.

What if I arose from slumber to know love all around me in a child's eyes, a lover's kiss, If I would only open my eyes.

What if I woke up when others were still asleep to see things differently, to see God as my own divinity.

What if I became aware of the places in my heart I had hidden to see the connection to all of humanity if only I would open my eyes to see.

What if I could see the inner light of divinity infinite and ever present that's been waiting for me to awaken to its intensity.

What if I woke up when others were still asleep and found a different world astonishing in beauty no longer hidden from me by my refusal to see.

What if from sleep I ceased from finding God out there and looked to see all I sought within me where its always been.

What if I woke up and could see the fuller more abundant life I thought had eluded me was there all along if I would but awaken to see.

What if I woke up when others were still asleep and it all became plain from slumber I'd chosen to hide my eyes to the wonder of my own luminosity.

Stillness

Before a cup is poured a dog barks, Stillness.

Before a rooster crows daylight breaks, Stillness.

Before work, love, play, Stillness.

Before caring, learning, doing, Stillness.

Before living, Stillness.

Dance of Two Souls

*A man a woman, two souls searching for the other,
the other for the one.*

*Two souls searching, waiting for the someday
when two souls become one.*

*Two souls from the shadows, one from the other,
the other from the one, the dance begins, the music
plays on.*

*Two souls together, years unfolded, hearts in
rhythm to life's song, a slow dance, two souls as
one.*

Old Self

Old self, must I remind you to no longer dwell in command of me, thoughts and feelings embedded so long to feel entitled to interrupt when new self speaks up.

Old self, new self must overcome your being to find truth in the harmony and order of the universe.

Old self, you persist to feel instilled, your fraud exposed by the truth of my will.

Old self, is it fear of losing control you've commanded all these years when new self was hidden.

Old self, is the fear of death to surely come when new self reigns for all to know the truth of who I am.

Abundance

*Abundance, surely we're to have all we want,
the universe to provide if we only believe we're
entitled.*

*Well I don't know, sounds too extravagant, better
to work hard and see what we can get if we're
fortunate enough to have it.*

*Wealth of many meanings, money, peace, joy,
love, happiness, all is ours and more of the good
provided, God's decree our right to have if we but
feel worthy of it.*

*Well I don't know, sounds unreal you know when
we remember where we came from, so poor we
were back then.*

*Abundance, Jesus said it best, he'd come that we
might have life and have it more abundantly.*

*Well I don't know, growing up it was best not to get
too big for our britches, you know what I mean.*

*Abundance, what can I say, but know best to let
the past be the past and change all thoughts of
unworthiness to a heart grateful for our abundant
inheritance.*

Love Spent

New wine, tender vines, love's embrace, love to spend.

Strong wine, fires touch, passions burn, love to spend.

Mellow wine, light breezes, embers glow, love to spend.

Aged wine, vows renewed, promises kept, love spent.

Morning Flight

Beautiful morning for a flight, sky blue, not a cloud in sight, only the colors of emerging daylight, hues of red and pink only the Master Artist could paint.

My little plane waits wings wet with morning dew she's rested through the night, engine cold, fluids settled from previous flight.

Skin shiny she's a real beauty, I could swear I saw her smile, waiting all the while for my return to bring to life, engine to turn, wings to lift, return to the skies where so many times with me she's been.

Preflight, sure to check it all can't miss a step, she'll take care of me if I do the prep.

Inside, we are one ready for flight strapped tightly in her grasp, soon to be free from earth's mighty grasp.

The runway appears ahead, disappears behind, wheels turn, wings lift, controls light, the way she feels such a delight.

We climb, steady 70 on the speed gauge, another measuring the rate, into the beauty of the morning light.

Sun's rays warm her cabin and my spirit stirs with anticipation forgetting I'm flying, procedures let go, eyes straight ahead, only this moment I know, just me and her climbing into the heavens.

Hand in Hand

*I turned the corner early morning, I believe, they
were there on the other side of the street, backs
to me, he and she short of stature, about the same
height, maybe a little slouched like me, hand in
hand their steps slow, a little old like me I could
see.*

*Morning walk to their delight, holding hands, I
thought so sweet of them and of my sweetie and
me as we often would be.*

*Maybe visiting the neighborhood, clad in bathrobes
his gray hers pink, each modestly closed, wrapped
tight at their waist above the knees.*

*Didn't seem to care about dress, the way they were
or what anyone might say about their morning
affair, walking in the neighborhood.*

*Hand in hand, listening only to the bliss they
shared in each others company that morning
together they seemed not to know "Where" or
"When" or even the "Why" of it, and I suppose
didn't much care.*

Lady of the Street

Lady of burden, old, stooped, worn, tattered, wrinkled, tangled hair.

Lady of the street, rusted cart, wheels bent, ragged clothes, street smells.

Lady of alleys, cans, bottles, discarded baubles and other treasures, fished from the detritus of the days trash.

Lady of shadows, night fears, lonely street, another night's cold sleep, wondering if dawn will come again to her street.

Flag Lady

*She's there alone every day dusty wind and hot
sun in her face, noise to withstand to keep traffic
controlled coming and going in her assigned road
construction area.*

*She's dressed for the part, blue jeans, work shirt,
cap venting a pony tail, dark glasses to shield a
pretty face, no makeup she needs.*

*She wields a traffic flag on a wooden pole royal
scepter to let cars stop or pass one way or the
other, she's in command, the Flag Lady.*

*She's on the job rain or shine with the noise the
dirt and the grime, angry drivers, barking dogs and
catcalls too, the Flag Lady.*

*She does her work uncomplaining, returning smiles
quick to say a word or two in passing, waving to
kids, blowing them a kiss when they wave back, the
Flag Lady.*

*She'd be somewhere else if she could, home with
kids of her own maybe, but for now she's content
to be there in her road construction area, the Flag
Lady.*

Life After Death

Life after death there's no guarantee of a heaven but certainly no hell either, would be against God's nature discerned of eternal love to destroy that which he created.

Oh, but what of sin you wonder, what to do with that, surely punishment for the unatoned, judgment day waiting for the last breath, but this cannot be counted either, even if to stumble and fall, for God's forgiveness of man's poor choices, freewill given to all.

Life after death, no one's returned with the definitive story, only personal revelations and intuition that something as lovely as a soul, no matter where its been, what its done or failed to learn, is still one of God's greatest treasures.

So may we conclude if we choose to know of life after death, we need look no further than the wonder and mystery of all creation from here to infinity of God's divine love.

And of all that's said and done about life hereafter there's this thought to consider of God the Master Painter, each of us a precious stroke on the canvas of his image, surely a work of art he'd never relinquish.

Good Old Love Making

*Sexual performance, knew that would get attention
but dear poet must you go there to dare open
the can of what, when, why, how and where in a
verse to demonstrate the absurdity of the sexual
revolution.*

*There was a time of course when love making was
much simpler, this thing of man and woman, before
the world became obsessed with body parts,
procedures and definitions.*

*But then as such things must advance, the experts
decided no one really knew much of it and best
instruction books be printed to set it all right, this
thing of day and night.*

*A revolution began with Mr. Kinsey who took
to task to research and experiment inhibition's
derivation, concluding we must evolve, the
missionary position would have to go.*

*Roles examined, scripts rewritten of positions,
some quite athletic, personal equipment to analyze,
measurements to be taken, names to assign,
questions of frequency, whether to crawl, walk or
run in sexual activity, all the more mechanical than
fun.*

*Of course the subject titillating, we bought into
exploration to right the wrongs of our perceptions,
but for some neurosis developed for fear of lack,
performance falling short before the reviews were
in.*

*New terms entered the Sexual Lexicon to further
complicate, premature this and delayed that, and
failure of the erector set, enough dysfunction to
torment the strongest libido of affliction to worry it
surely could happen.*

*But to set minds at ease a new field developed,
sexual therapy for a price, could fix any malady
between the sheets with a pill, a shot, a device or
an Ink Blot Test, sure to heal the problem we never
knew we had.*

*Well, my poet friend, now you've done it, spoke
your piece and had some fun, but time moves on
and hard to say what's right or wrong as it's such
an individual thing, this sexual Inclination, but
for those of an older generation we got along just
fine before the revolution believing we were quite
advanced making love with the lights on.*

*"If you really want to know someone,
all you have to do is look,"
paraphrased from the movie, "Wonder."*

The Speaker

*He got up to speak, pushed his chair in where
it began, didn't seem nervous at the task ahead
speaking in front of an audience of likeminded
peers his story to reveal for all to hear.*

*I watched him close glad it him and not me who got
up to speak that evening long ago, for I knew his story
difficult to tell and I'd rather just listen if you will.*

*He made his way to the podium, walked too fast
in a hurry I thought to tell his story or maybe just
nervousness he displayed.*

*I watched him close, not an easy feeling the burden
I knew he carried pounding in his chest of the story
he'd come to tell that evening long ago, the man's
willingness to share innermost thoughts of a most
intimate nature.*

*He arrived on stage at the assigned place, the role to
assume but hesitated a moment to adjust his glasses,
removing his hearing aids for some unfounded
reason of modulation his voice constricted.*

*The audience waited as he began, the words a bit
stilted but nevertheless their meaning to ring of the
story he came to tell, in silence sat those who came
to hear.*

"Met a man not long ago on a mountain top," he began, said he knew me from the beginning and was glad I'd finally arrived where he sat atop a rock in a beautiful meadow of wild flowers, Aspen Trees and a slow-moving stream.

The opening sentence delivered, the audience riveted, he knew he had their attention as he searched their faces and noticed all eyes on him looking back.

So, the man I met looked a lot like me, he continued, but older, wiser and calmer, waiting there the many years I'd been absent, the audience murmured, some frowned a little puzzled.

The man told me he knew of my struggles playing the role of the script written by others and why it had taken so long to climb up where he'd waited for me to find the truth of myself.

The words gave him pause, he said, and he questioned what could be done at this late date of life to rewrite the script, rearrange the scenes of the role he'd played all those years.

It was then, he said, the man on the rock shifted his weight, reached inside a backpack beside him to produce a big book, grinning in anticipation as he handed it to me, stating this is your life between the pages from the womb to now for you to rewrite for a happier ending.

I reached for the book, he said, eager to begin knowing just the changes I'd make when the man said, "Not so fast," unwilling to release it just yet, rules to follow must be explained."

I felt disappointed wanting to begin, the speaker said, but knew the man he'd met was in control, the audience again murmured, "I believe he's right you know."

The man said I'd most benefit if not to change the events, the actors, or the roles they played, but only my part of the script I'd be allowed to rewrite.

And so he rewrote the script and did all the man had asked of him and when finished with the new role he'd play, knew it was only the beginning, the first of many steps he'd take on the journey to find the truth of himself one day.

Then his piece said, the speaker gathered his papers and returned to his seat believing he'd done his best to explain his encounter with himself on the mountaintop and the irony of the story of the past to heal a new script must be written.

I watched the speaker return to take his seat, knowing the pain of his journey of the previous script, but knew the spiritual journey he'd found would lead him to the truth of himself, who he was and had always been.

Trash Truck Man

The Trash Truck Man known to all in his weekly
forays, a lot of stops winding through the
neighborhood, forest of trashcans there for him to
pick up, some large, some small, some not there at
all, trash day forgotten.

He's short of stature but big of heart, knows a
thing or two about the mechanics of the huge truck
he operates to make a living he first must stop,
hop out to lift the small and manhandle the larger,
retrieve anything spilled from the cans.

The man I've come to watch and admire, dexterity
a flowing move could be a dancer waltzing his
subject up in his arms a tight squeeze into the bin,
the lever he pulls and the machinery grinds, the
trash pushed back and compacted, the can arriving
back on the ground where it began all in one swift
motion.

Then back in the cab to drive more cans awaiting
to repeat the tasks in order all over again, surely
must get tired the man's a warrior, the streets his
battlefields of neighborhoods all over town the
truck to fill of the town's trash.

He smiles a lot, friendly too the trash truck driver never fails to say hello to those he meets attending to their trash, wears a ball cap proud to advertise his company pulled down tight on the back of his head.

And so the day comes of a morning when what remains of all consumed the week before is not so neatly placed along the streets in the good hands of the Trash Truck Man.

My Grandson

*I watched him back then my grandson to play the
role of a policeman in the play he was in, so calm
and poised delivering each line with ease as if the
stage was meant to be for him.*

*Now again this night in a different play the actor a
teenager becoming a man, I thought of all that went
before this night to make us so proud of him.*

*It began, the baby in my arms watching over him
for the first six months of life when my daughter
returned to work part time, changing his diapers
and holding him close while he napped so
peacefully on my lap.*

*Then fast forward a few years and he's a toddler
around our house when mom and dad needed
a break, curious as all get out about everything,
words, colors, numbers, planets, books of every
kind we'd read, he'd ask, "Why" endlessly.*

*He liked coming over to grandpa and grandma's
house where he knew he'd be spoiled, catering to
his every whim with plenty of ice cream and we'd
be sure not to tell mom how late he stayed up at
night.*

A few more years and he and grandpa would play his little boy games, showing up in the costumes of fantasy, Superman, Spider man, Darth Vader or a Jedi Knight, we'd never know of whom he'd appear.

We played in the park running races and he always won of course and on our walks he'd be fascinated with ants and grasshoppers and when too far we'd wander, he'd be up on grandpa's shoulders to carry home.

We'd play his games in the neighborhood, chasing the bad guys, our Light Sabers rattling, bringing out the child in me and the hero in him.

We had great times pushing him on a swing or chasing geese at the park, grandpa's little red truck he enjoyed, sometimes on my lap he'd sit and steer around the parking lot, our secret safe from mom and dad.

Mom and dad thought it time about then to get him involved in sports, prevalent even among the little kids and he began on a soccer team to do his best, every Saturday morning the family gathered with great expectations of the next star to emerge from the pack of other kids like him.

He'd try and try with all his heart up and down the field to get the hang of it, we'd cheer him on to make the next pass, kick or the goal we hoped he could, his gentle soul a little reticent to mix it up.

*The seasons wore on and each year older he'd
advance with others his age, different team names,
Tigers, Badgers, Wolverines and he'd try hard to
shine in there for every play doing his best.*

*More years passed all too quickly it seemed and
next in his athletic excursions would be basketball
every Saturday, we'd all be there to cheer him on,
pass the ball, score a basket we knew he could
each time he tried.*

*Indoor football was next and he never faltered
or got discouraged, despite our exaggerated
expectations hoping he'd catch a pass or score a
touchdown in a bit of frenzy we'd work ourselves
up, his achievements few but he'd never let himself
down.*

*He'd continue to play sports through the middle
school years happy to be second fiddle, the first
to tell you of learning more than scoring goals or
making touchdowns or baskets in the gym, it was
the fun and teamwork that pleased him.*

*Then something new caught his eye and his spirit
soared of acting he'd try, mom encouraging him, all
of us would attend without expectations surprised
at the stellar performances he turned in.*

*A special school he'd attend his middle years
quite advanced in math and science but nothing
of drama or social exchange there for him to enjoy
before the traditional high school opened a new
world for him with social life and drama, plays of
life to star in.*

Best Friend

When we wed I got more than I'd bargained for and glad I did because you see when you became my wife, dear, you also became my best friend.

Okay, so it didn't happen right away with the issues of newlyweds to work out, our spaces together to explore limits and when to back off and let the other come out.

The days, months and years went by and we knew our destiny together was clear, but it was only later we'd discover for better or worse we'd be each other's friend.

And so, when I came to you with a problem or you did the same with me, it wasn't advice we'd get from a husband-wife perspective, but a hand to hold or a pat on the back that said, "I hear you my friend."

And when we'd falter, me or you, we'd never hear, "I told you so," but only, "It's okay," I am here to help you when you go astray.

And the mistakes we made they were many on both sides of the union but we learned at times like that, that it wasn't the critic we heard but the voice of the best friend.

So my dear, all I can say and must is the wife I knew you to be always there to love, care and support me, was all the sweeter made to know the best friend was there too.

Thank you, Dad

Thank you, Dad not for who you were but for who you wanted to be free of fear and doubt to see the truth of the man you could be.

It wasn't much fun being your son I must say but thank you anyway for the better side of yourself you hid in despair, the side I couldn't see but knew must be there.

Thank you, Dad for who you wanted to be, your divine self to find but never would, the stars failed to decree for you to see the truth of yourself, your spirit forever hidden.

Our days together quickly passed, I progressed despite the pain of our past, your long shadow over me cast, to escape in the truth revealed to me of my authentic being, the opposite of who I thought I should be.

Caught up in you I was smothered not by the love which you could not give but by the man I thought you were and I tried to be, the man you had falsely modeled for me.

Your addiction to the vices of your choosing, not wrong in themselves but only as you used them to hide the fears of the man you were afraid to be.

We went our separate ways as fathers and sons do, you forever to search for the man behind the pain, the mental struggle you fought so hard to understand, despairing to your last breath of finding the source of your darkness within.

Night Comes

*Night comes as it must tip toeing on tender feet
calling me to unwind the thoughts collected
in my wakefulness stored from the day's
subconsciousness to keep me awake.*

*Night deepens to realize the tempest in my soul
rising like a gathering wind to swirl and dance the
nightly game of torment of things long past to spoil
a good night's rest.*

*Night evolves as the Cosmos directs true to
laws the heavens bless, stars out to shine the
universe well meaning, calling me to lay upon
the bed of peace to let go the things preventing
sleep.*

*Sleep but moments away it must be I delight,
eyelids heavy, breathing rhythmic I will my mind to
quiet the voices turbulent, a switch to be found to
make them go away.*

*Now darkness deepens as it must, but absence
of light fails of its promise to release me to the
night, minutes become more, time marches out
of step with each toss and turn to wrestle from
the demons who would have their way at my
resistance.*

*No laughing matter it is to be deprived of rest by
this tempest raging, waves of torment breaking
over my mind dousing the gentle flame of sleep
dissolving in ashes of agitation.*

*Wee hours of morning arrive, too quickly of course,
brief moments unable to stretch nodding off to
find a dream to record in the log of another night's
restlessness.*

Mornings

Why can't mornings last all day bright promise of life anew vibrant freshness of renewal summoned from night's sleep, must afternoons and evenings come their story so humdrum, void of mornings blessings.

Why can't mornings last all day would some dreadful thing occur if it were to always be the morning of today before the morning of tomorrow, if mornings were to last past noon would only breakfast suffice, lunch and dinner never to be served, only mornings of light, pleasing sounds, sweet smells of delight.

Why can't mornings last all day, would it hurt for the morning to emerge from the dark night past to last to the next day's morning its brightness cast, why can't mornings last all day.

Sacred Spirits

Sacred spirits move across the great lands of sage and brush where once Buffalo thundered for as far as can be seen by those who now pass the lands long forgotten, living ghosts of long ago hidden in the hardness of time, their voices heard if you but listen.

The land now traversed by concrete, striped and smoothed for conveyance of time and place, modern passage from lowlands to mountain peaks where people play at modern life in forms of recreation.

Sacred spirits voices of then live today in more than memory of a great spiritual land held in destiny's plan of unrequired redemption not to fear but to be heard if you but listen.

These same spirits strayed beyond the great expanse of man's memory, advancing and retreating as they wished, winding through the mountains and hills, stopping only for streams to pass, you may hear them still if you but listen.

Sacred spirits tell a story of times past in the changing winds of voices long forgotten but never lost as they passed through the bloodshed of wars still to be heard if you but listen.

*Across the open expanse of life past and present
my spirit sacred through the years and now to
be heard by those who would not fear or lack
understanding or appreciation of the wholeness of
the life I too traveled across these lands.*

Spilled Water

*From a medical meeting we had come mid-morning
and still not eaten, thoughts of surgery scheduled
soon my mind possessed.*

*Stopped at a place where we'd seldom been for a
bite and time to decompress from thoughts of all
that had just taken place and all still ahead feeling
a bit like wishing it didn't have to happen.*

*The waitress we had drawn or maybe she'd drawn
us appeared to serve and cater to our needs,
pleasant enough I thought, but something within
me wanted to know more of who she was and why
she was there.*

*Older than usual for the job, was she retired and
needing the work or working elsewhere and filling
in here, requirements of family needs to meet.*

*She seemed to try, but the smile was lacking
only revealing what she deemed to show, holding
something in the shadows of her being no stranger
with thoughts of surgery on his mind could ever
know.*

*She took care of business at our table, and our food
arrived to our satisfaction, but in her hurry managed
to spill a glass of water, sorry the look on her face
and the word from her mouth of the situation.*

I assured her no reason to worry or be sorry, I wasn't the type to be offended even though I'd had my shower for the day, I kidded, and maybe detected the slightest of smiles as she cleaned up the mess.

Time moved on and our breakfast finished, she returned to see if we needed anything more, this waitress I had begun to know but yet so much remained hidden in her demeanor to enquire of as I'm often to do.

Learned some things but of course I'd never know of her journey of life or a spiritual path I'd have liked to discern of what I saw in her and what I saw of her in myself there in her midst.

We left as it was time to go, myself to return again from the brief encounter therein to the thoughts and concerns of surgery, her story in my preoccupation, receding from my mind.

I told her she had done a great job and wished her well wanting her to see the possibilities within herself of a broader smile at life's little complexities, spilling water but a trifle at best.

Leave her a big tip my inner voice said, don't entertain whether she needs it or not and write upon the bill, "Thank you! You did a great job," for her to see we're all one in this big beautiful sea of spilled water at breakfast.

Today's the Day

Today's the day I've heard it said, the anniversary of when we wed fifty-five years ago, can't help but remember when we knelt in agreement that our lives would be forever one.

Today's the day we set aside, marked on the calendar of our lives not so much to recreate but to reflect of blessings we've been graced to redeem from the victories and defeats, the laughs and tears through which we've lived our lives.

Today's the day, there's none other to look one another in the eyes and say, "Thank You Dear" for one year more of the pleasure of your presence, the love you freely give, the smile shining bright upon the face reflected for the other to see.

Today's the day we celebrate and rightly so for there's much to honor, much to appreciate of the story we've written from the fabric of life woven with the intention, purpose, and care of our lives together we've chosen to live.

Today's the day we celebrate, not much more to say of it, words inadequate by any measure of how great its been, is, and will be each year again.

Lady of the Sea

She's trim from bow to stern, amidships too, rigged and ready for the biggest blow, a little boat steady as she sails the storm that refuses to let go.

Must admire her mettle high in the water she rides with ease, her main taut of the shouting wind, jib responding in kind full speed ahead proving her worth as fine a sailing boat as there's ever been.

Her helm responds as it's wont to do taking commands from the wind's direction, shifts of quarter, abeam and stern this day of stormy insurrection.

Waves breaking as mountain tops capped with foam, a rogue or two to test the lady's strength in the toughest storm she's encountered close hauled on chosen tack, captain of her fate.

Darkness obstructs the way ahead out of sight of land, she's holding as best she can, assault of wind and angry sea, agony in her beams fore and aft to withstand never to complain of her plight through the day and through the unrelenting night.

Her soul fights for control the best of intention, hellish waves breaking in rapid succession over her bow descending to purgatory to rise again to the door of heaven.

Should she last the night the current rigging under too much sail, no time to reef, sea anchor lacking, she'll be afloat come morning's first light.

Waves furious to blow Force 10 show her no respect knocked down from a mighty one, what's up is down, what's down is up, watery overhead, dry deck in opposing positions before righting herself again.

How much more the question begs, not to plead, can she take before she's forced from the fight withdrawn, bright light of resolve extinguished, committed to the depth of the sea's taking.

She's dying It's plain to see floundering in a misery of the saddest fate for a lady so gallant when on the horizon a sliver of dawn breaks across her bow, wind letting go of its bluster for now.

The lady of the night worn and weary, but intact to lay claim to life redeemed from her tormentor of the night, to sail again a new day.

"When you want something, all the universe conspires to help you achieve it," Paulo Coelho, *"The Alchemist"*

Where Was God?

*The day's news again brings sadness, another
shooting horrific, weather devastation, lost
lives and lives injured, families grieving not
understanding why life was from them suddenly
taken, leaving them to ask, "Why," and where was
God in all of this?*

*Another day, always seems too soon, terrorism
afflicts in fanaticism against cherished values
and way of life, carnage strewn in the aftermath
of another senseless act, left to ask, "Why," and
where was God in all of this?*

*There's a reprieve and lives begin to heal, we're
told we're safe and all will be well, vivid images
fade from the minds of those resilient against
the harsh realities of the tragic past, but still the
question remains to ask, "Why," and where was
God in all of this?*

*Why indeed, and where was God when it seemed
hell had once again reigned, evil triumphant yet
again the question pleads to answer why we feel
so forsaken, the faith of a most ardent believer
shaken.*

Still the answer eludes us of understanding beyond the pain and misery of inhumanity to human kind, difficult when sought through troubled minds, but should we dare inquire, may be found within us of God's presence in the midst of all that's bloody, broken and forsaken.

Hard to believe and certainly need to question but consider God was there from the beginning in the one scared and in panic who covered another in protection, the first responder a moment removed from sanity, in harm's way summoning the courage to save life and limb, the skilled ready to receive the trauma delivered to them, the unity of survivors and friends to comfort and reassure, a charitable nation's response overwhelming.

There's more of course to speak of God in the midst, the seen and unseen of his hand best understood perhaps not in the moment of anguish, but in looking back one day in appreciation of all the good that came out of it.

A Brother

I have a brother I believe him to be, but a nephew I suppose in reality's deception, a son of my sister who came to be my mother's love instead of me.

Separated by chance or human transgression, who's to say, but more inclined to belief of divine intervention did the universe ordain a sister's son become a mother's love instead of me.

The brother I call Timothy I've come to love in a spiritual sense, our souls blessed with gifts of creativity, music of him, the written word of me, mined from lives lived of the depths of life's uncertainties where true notes and words are best expressed.

Life most interesting and unique can best be seen from within, reflection of divine oneness discerned to conspire my sister's son become my mother's love instead of me.

Spirit Guides

*Spirit Guides I've been told I have and believe
it must be true as I've felt protected, directed,
overseen, annoyed, prodded, poked and nudged at
times for reasons known only to them.*

*I have more than one, of course, seven really, hope
they're not offended, the names of dwarfs I've
given them, Doc, Happy, Grumpy, Sneezy, Dopey,
Bashful and Sleepy from Snow White legend.*

*Doc appears when a pain I believe must be
something serious, mind reeling much too fast
in hypochondria's grasp, to poke me in the ribs,
shake my shoulders, my attention to get, let me
know he's not kidding.*

*Happy, his jolly self around most of the time my
best friend it seems to change my mood when it
lapses, reminding me of life's beauty still here,
there, everywhere to see.*

*Grumpy, the darnedest old cuss, don't know why
he shows up when I'm feeling weary or out or sorts,
must be to help me see the state I'm in is just a
reflection of him.*

Sneezy arrives with a sheepish grin usually in springtime his fun to have at my expense, my head of pollen reeling, sneezing with each breath until he suddenly disappears again.

Dopey can be such a pest reminding me of the absurdity of behavior, outrageousness of life when I feel a little too serious, to get a little crazy, have a little fun, be a little foolish the little guy insists.

Bashful, I really don't hear from him much since childhood days but sometimes he shows up to protect my ego when I cower in the shadows of uncertainty, moving in until I dispel his reticent behavior.

Sleepy, he arrives too without notice when I need most to be alert for a task to complete in record time, reminds of the slower pace I'm apt to find if I would only listen to him.

So, there you see my spirit guides examined in jest and of course mislabeled, nothing else to describe their presence when least expected, Doc, Happy, Grumpy, Sneezy, Dopey, Bashful and Sleepy, hope they're not offended.

Hearts and Souls of Love

Hearts and souls of love seeking and being sought in the divine plan of union of woman and man, reasons many and varied visible and invisible to find and be found.

Hearts aflame with passion, roadblock of distortion, shadows of fantasies beholden of intention the way lost too easily in distraction.

Hearts questionings, yearnings and needs inner directed from love's place the surer path in love's direction if to find the opposite kind of such seeking.

Minds raging with answers before there's questions, sure to implode in anticipation of solace of the struggle within of belief of being to withstand scrutiny of another's discretion.

Lonely souls all too vulnerable find the easiest path through the heart's maze of indiscretion, first in love and first to fall out, once and many times again.

Playful the hearts that tug and pull the strings, messages teasing, not always pleasing, naïve of love's ways, lacking sophistication.

Best the heart by far which knows well the depth of its soul's lacking, that only the object of its longing with love would fill.

God of Love

God of love, fabric of life woven in infinite creation, wholeness and harmony of divine presence, perfection of form celestial and earthly life found in the narrow and extreme, the greatest the smallest inclusive a people's choice good or evil but of love the better, a mother's caring, a child's smile, helping hand extended, the bulb seeded in winter to blossom in spring,

I too my soul joyous one with what is and has always been creation united in love, wholeness and harmony, life without limit, fullness beyond measure, love unconditioned to forever treasure.

I declare love and benevolence worthy of mine to own and purvey of beloved perfection, abundance overflowing, freedom to live from truth of being, freedom to know oneness infinitely within.

Gratefulness the universe sings for its nature one in all and all in one the thankful heart to feel thanksgiving and appreciation of eternal expression divinely given throughout time.

The taste of glory sweet on the tongue of discovery, but not to languish or be enamored if to be returned is first released to the law's doing to be so and so to be, Amen.

Floyd's Barbershop

Gather around my fellow men of mustaches, beards and hair on your heads, there's just the place for you to go, two streets down and around the corner, can't miss the striped pole out front of Floyd's Barbershop, all your needs there to be met, even a man with a rag if you've a hankering for shoes to shine.

Old Floyd's the proprietor a man of color with a smile as broad as the street outside, and a big belly full of laughter, he'll tell you of his trade he learned as a boy of nine or ten from his daddy, even bigger, in Mississippi in a little town along the river where the days were hot and the fishing better.

Now Floyd's made a name for himself since arriving where he's at, opening the little shop two streets down and around the corner with the striped pole out front and several more barbers of color, the sign on the door, "Floyd's Barber Shop, Welcome, Come on in."

But it's Floyd who'll greet you when you drop by, ask you "How you doing friend," smile as wide as the street outside and a laugh from his big belly, make you feel at home, want to stay awhile even if only to shoot the bull, always a chair or two there just for you.

*Now any day if you'd happen by, you'll hear the
place a rocking with the music Floyd likes to play,
and the men in the chairs and those waiting talking
about the weather, the high school football team
losing again and Floyd a bragging about the fish
he'd caught just the other day but had caught
bigger ones where he'd been.*

*So, guess there's not much more to say of Floyd of
where he's from and where he's been, but of the life
in him he hands out with the haircuts, shaves and
mustache trims at the little shop two streets down
and around the corner, the striped pole outside
and the sign on the door that says, "Floyd's Barber
Shop, Welcome, Come on in."*

Misguided Journey

The day's events transpired to trouble this tender heart of performance misguided in anxiety's grasp.

The journey with others dependent was not of the usually sure and steady hand but of fear's reign over trust and confidence, judgment hindered, slow to react to uncertainty ahead.

Was nothing too serious that occurred, misnomers of procedures mostly no real harm done, fellow travelers may have not even noticed more than one or two indiscretions.

The journey's end is now since past from day to night of what had unraveled of calm deliberation, characteristic steady hand.

The travelers have gone off to live in their individual selves, not remembering transgressions or believing them of much import.

But still the tender heart troubled of its tapes to replay and relive to not let go of irresponsibility or realize imperfection.

Tomorrow will come and many thereafter this day's events to fade away, the self to mend the critic to find work elsewhere.

Morning Comes

*Morning comes and light absent through the
dark night steals through and around the drapes
of the bedroom window, arousing me if only
subconsciously from sleep.*

*My mind yawns, soon to catch on to buy what
the new day is selling to awaken me and my eyes
follow its direction, resisting maybe but knowing
it is time to wake from the night's dreams to begin
yet another day's imperfections.*

*I am hesitant to get up to leave the confines of the
warm cocoon which has embraced me through the
night as a child between birth and life and I toss
and turn a few times in my hesitation.*

*The light which began its dance of reflection steps
up its pace fed by the morning's position, turning
in my direction and I'm inclined to sit up and my
legs let dangle off the bed.*

*I rub my eyes, the mind of today not yet working
and delight in a sacred moment between sleep and
arising from bed when life is still, no voices yet of
worry or concern planning for the day to discern
somewhere in the midst of a moment so still and
calm I wish never to relinquish.*

The moment fades all too soon and all the things it held back for that brief respite, come rushing forth again so I should not sit here much longer in this space, but rise to accept the new day of life to begin.

I will my feet to know once again their place in all of this to carry me from the bed to wherever my mind need take me but as I yawn and rub my eyes, I can't but wonder if all day long I could live in that moment when nothing mattered but silence between sleep and awakening.

Eldon Gurnis

*Eldon Gurnis, meanest old man in Champaign
County, a farmer I once knew, worked for him a
long time ago when I was young and failed the test
of the way he wanted things done.*

*Old Eldon stood about five feet ten and weighed
too much for his height, a farmer all his life in
Ohio's lands, a wife so sweet much in contrast to
him.*

*He'd give me the tasks out around the barn to move
the hay, cut the weeds, clean out the manure, tell
me each day when I'd come around, a mile there
and a mile back home again.*

*Eldon could be contrary, a life so long of hard work
and upbringing couldn't be happy with what I did
making me do it over again, face red from the sun
or maybe rage, never knew, swearing up a storm
for emphasis he could do.*

*Sometimes I'd walk the mile and show up early in
the morning, his wife to answer the door, Eldon's
out in the fields she'd say, said to get you started
out around the barn, move the hay, cut the weeds
and clean out the manure.*

*He'd come along later on the big John Deere
he'd maneuver in front of the barn where I'd been
hoping he'd notice the fine job I'd done moving
the hay, cutting the weeds and cleaning out the
manure.*

*But Old Eldon, never one for praise, just didn't
find it in his nature not to find fault aplenty with
the way the hay was moved, the weeds were cut
and the manure removed, swearing up a storm for
emphasis he could do.*

*He never wanted me around to help milk the cows
or feed the pigs, I never knew why, and would have
welcomed the diversity and opportunity to have
been of help to him.*

*But as it was I was resigned each day to the barn to
move the hay, cut the weeds, clean out the manure,
a mile there and a mile back, he'd be as mean as
the day before, swearing up a storm for emphasis
he could do.*

*I have to say as a young boy of fourteen, a day
never went by when I wasn't fearful the way he'd
keep me hopping, his sweet wife when she had a
chance to get me aside, would say, don't pay him
no matter, just the way he is.*

*Days went by that summer, the work hot and
sweaty in the barn and thereabouts moving the hay,
cutting the weeds and cleaning out the manure,
but my first job I wanted to do good, so told myself
to just put up with him, walking a mile there and a
mile back home again.*

The Man in the Chair

Passing by, couldn't help but stop, had to talk, at least say, "Hi."

Don't know what attracted me, what appeal did I see, bushy eyebrows, fair skin, average build, nothing special about him, must have been the way he looked at me.

I said, "Hi," he said, "Good morning," greetings exchanged, tell me about your day, Oh, up at five, two-mile walk you see, now resting here where you have found me.

No morning mine to match that, I thought, short bike ride around the loop down the path and back to where he sat.

A pleasant exchange, couldn't help but feel serenity's presence as he'd look off between our words, a distant place in mind, a minute or maybe two, a mile away or more, vision or memory of a distant reflection.

Firmly planted in the presence of the moment, I allowed him to ponder his look off yonder and patiently wait for a response on his own good time of his return from wherever he went on a journey of inspiration.

Lonely Lady

*"Excuse me sir," she said, "may I get by on the way
to a movie seat beyond where you sit."*

*Nothing unusual about that but had to wonder if
another lady or gentleman, son or daughter would
follow the "Excuse Me Lady" to the seat beside her
to sit, someone close, maybe a friend, spouse or
lover, someone, anyone to share the movie with.*

*A reasonable time I waited to check again,
dismayed no one had taken the place next to where
she sat, even a stranger at this point would do,
how sad I thought, though she may not agree or
welcome the thought not to sit alone with no one to
share the movie with.*

*Had I been brave, I'd stepped down the row to
where the "Excuse Me Lady" sat, leaned over and
in my best "Excuse Me Man" voice asked if she'd
care beside her I might sit.*

*The moment of daring passed, thoughts were
another place, the "Excuse Me Lady" on her own,
I left to regret what might have been if I'd acted,
maybe the "Excuse Me Lady" and the "Excuse Me
Man" would have sat side by side the movie or
something more of life to share.*

The movie over, again she passed by me excusing herself once more, a smile I detected of thought of mind she may have had of, "What if I'd taken the seat next to him to share the movie with."

*"...I am the master of my fate,
I am the captain of my soul," Invictus*

Oh, Ohio

*Oh, Ohio, I tried to let you go, but you wouldn't
let go of me, thoughts of then so long ago to stir
memories, some good but more unwanted to haunt
rather than please.*

*Must I continue to entertain the schools of
disappointment a young boy's experiences lost in
impermanence of another's restlessness of those
years long ago.*

*And of the many places called home, the towns,
cities and rural areas surrounded by farms where
I'd find summer work baling hay, I still hold so
tightly to thoughts I thought were gone.*

*And of the many friends I had but knew only by
points recorded in the games we played and the
loves of back then now leaves loose in the wind of
what might have been.*

*Oh, Ohio, you filled me to the brim with your
essence, summer rains, torrents of horrific
thunder, seasons to change overnight, the
sudden smell of spring, sweet freshness barely
removed from the days of heavy wraps and snow
balls to heave.*

*And the people you surrounded me with,
some gifts of the universe, others a burden, a
grandmother's love and care, others caught in the
confusion of the roles they played with scripts they
failed to read.*

*Oh, Ohio, you took me from my mother's womb so
innocent and worked your way with me of place
where so much happened happy and sad a trail of
laughter and tears the good and the bad.*

*And now I'm much older and chase after the stars
not seeking retribution or needing resolution for
time has taken care of that, but to know the place
of myself I've always been, the truth lost and found,
but which could never go home again.*

*Oh, Ohio, you've been a mixed blessing home
of much to cherish, but much more left behind,
lifetime of thoughts and memories carried in my
mind of all that came before the day I tried to let
you go.*

*Oh, Ohio, I believed my mind to erase the images
and feelings of discontent of those years in your
embrace, but somewhere in the wonder and
mystery of the distant past you decreed it never to
last.*

I'll Just Be

I think today I'll just "Be", what do you think of that, I'm sure you have an opinion.

How could I just "Be" even for one day you wonder with so much required of me to not just "Be".

No, I must try to give it a go when fear comes a crawling I'll say, "How do you do, but just toddle off somewhere else you see this is my day to just "Be".

I believe I'll just "Be" when thoughts try to get the best of me, don't they see they haven't a chance now that I've decided to just "Be".

And when I feel offended by some slight imagined, I'll just shrug it off to come another day this one taken, I'll just "Be".

Surely the universe has much to give and I'll accept not in supplication but with who I am and my preference in the grand procession to just "Be".

And if today to just "Be" works according to plan and happier I am to do all I must against my adversaries and trust my plan, I'll just "Be" and then tomorrow I'll just "Be" all over again.

Learning Spanish

Muchas Gracias Senor Amigo the words rolled off my tongue and the poor confused object of my Spanish lesson looked amused and began to laugh, something amiss in my dialect he'd found.

My journey of a foreign language began when I thought I'd be smart and learn a few words to converse with the Mexican restaurant waiters and waitresses, the lawn care taker, the trash truck driver or anyone of the heritage I thought would listen.

I found a book of translations and went to work on the basics, Gracias, Muchas and Mucho, Amigo, Como Esta Usted, Bueno, and a few others of course to show my new Spanish intellect.

So when the waiter came I was ready, Como Esta Usted was my how are you and he'd reply," Bueno" very good we really had it going I could see how fluent I'd become.

But a few words more and I was done my vocabulary exhausted left only to revert to my native tongue, but not bad I thought he must be charmed I'd tried to speak some of the language native to him.

*It didn't always go as well, however, when I'd open
my mouth and the right form of the word I'd fail to
remember, let's see were ladies Amigas or Amigos,
men Amigos or Amigas and was it Muchas or
Mucho Gracias.*

*In the confusion and chaos created not knowing
day from night or Senoras from Senoritas, they
were quick to correct, and my better half would
roll her eyes and simply say cut it out, you'll get in
trouble and whatever you do don't order Huevos
for breakfast, you may get testicles instead.*

*I tried it wherever Hispanics were employed
and was getting better, even got through a few
sentences with the trash truck driver but then the
day I passed a homeless man on the street I knew
I was done with this linguistic adventure when I
heard myself say, "Buenos Dias Senor," he had the
good courtesy to laugh and relate, "I don't speak
Spanish, Mister."*

Son or Daughter

Son or daughter, a worthy conundrum of us who've had one or the other to consider the treasures of our boy or girl yet difficult the question to answer only to ponder the rich blessings of one or the other.

Only I may speak of the daughter I'm happy to have a gift of God's choosing after deliberation of just the right fit but to know if he'd chosen differently and it had been a boy, a son I'd have loved no less.

Son or daughter of which is favored by those who say it doesn't matter, but rare the dad who in his secret place doesn't wish for the buddy to play catch or go fishing with.

And rare the mother in her feminine whiles does not wish for a daughter to nurture in the ways of becoming a woman, and the father just as happy to have the daughter to teach in his protection of the ways of men.

And so we come to the end of this verse, the question, son or daughter unanswered here and now, but may best be known if destiny permits mom and dad to have one of each.

Fiesta Santa Fe

Fiesta!

*Celebration festive comes once a year to Santa Fe,
the Plaza in the city decorative and gay, natives
and guests for a week to play chasing gloom from
their midst, Fiesta on their lips.*

*Old Man Zozobra of custom handed down through
the years to be set aflame burns away gloom that
happiness may reign and Fiesta begin.*

*When the ashes grow cold, natives and guests
fill the large expanse of grass with benches
for visitors to rest, the Bandstand readied for
Mariachis to play attired in beaded pants, button
coats and big Sombreros to wear, smiles as wide
as New Mexico canyons, music to bring Fiesta
alive.*

*The ladies too are there for fun young and old,
children too, beautiful as a sunset, they dance and
strut in hoop skirts and blousy blouses, Tiaras to
shine, the dancing and twirling festive divine.*

*There's more of course, always is, for the natives
know how to put on a show, food carts, oh so many
encircle the Plaza with delicacies and treats, New
Mexican fare, Enchiladas, Tortillas, Tacos and the
state cookie Biscochitos, the list goes on, salty*

Corn on the Cob dipped in butter, ice cream and soda pop at many of the stands, something for every palate to delight in.

And should the revelers take to the streets, and they do, restaurants and shops they find open for eats, trinkets, and souvenirs to own, but there's more yet to enjoy, always is, music in the air everywhere, vendors to show and sell their wares, jewelry and crafts made throughout the year fashioned as only they can, heritage of artisan's blood in their past.

And, there's more, as there always is, vendors stretch for blocks along side streets, tents filled with those who would look and those who would buy, the curious and wise, something for everyone to enjoy.

And so, my friends if you've been attentive, gather around for one more verse, and open your minds and hearts as well to Fiesta's enchantment, Old Man Zozobra, dancers, music makers, food carts and vendors, images to hold in your minds so dear until Fiesta comes around again next year.

Firetruck

*And so my friend and neighbor do you want to
know how to get a firetruck here, coming roaring
up lights a blazing, sirens screaming, I can make
one appear right here in a few minutes before your
very eyes.*

*I know your mind is trying to discern my crazy idea
of making a fire truck appear, you must think I have
a trick up my sleeve or to pull it from a magic hat,
but it's really quite simple and I'll explain all that.*

*The trick I learned some time ago quite by accident
you see one morning I awoke quite groggy and
attempted to disarm the security alarm, but it didn't
go quite according to plan, which I'll explain.*

*I fumbled with the buttons not really awake and
happened to push one I'd not tried before, you see,
and didn't pay too much attention in my sleepy
state when something about a fire alarm displayed.*

*The alarm disarmed, I went about my business
trying to shake off the confusion when not long
thereafter a banging on the door I heard and when
I answered there were three of the town's finest
firemen ready to enter, a fire to put out they thought
they were there for.*

After the shock wore off and I gathered my wits enough to let them have a look about and apologized rather profusely for the false alarm I'd created in my stupor to disarm pushed the fire alarm button instead.

So my friend and neighbor you see it's really quite simple to make a fire truck appear if in a groggy state of confusion your fingers wander too far astray to miss the disarm and land on the fire alarm button I wouldn't recommend, and have since covered it over so as not to ever again make a firetruck appear in the early morning hours for the neighbors to see.

Essence

I say learned friend, student of the book of wisdom and all things spiritual, I pose a question I've found no answer of what is the essence of one to linger when going about from place to place, from here to there, from there to here, anywhere from where one chooses to vacate or locate.

The essence of which I speak, invisible substance of heart, spirit, soul of being, the sense of the vacated physical presence left behind.

It often occurs to me of someone leaving my presence, the essence of them lingers and trust it's true of when I leave them if they care to explore the quintessence of my totality of mind, body and spirit that remains when I leave.

And, what of a closet of clothes I wonder if not the senses to discern the wearer's essence long after they have been worn and hung back on the shelf before they are worn again.

So, friend, if you've a mind to peruse the book of spiritual knowledge, not the proven or doubted but the mystery and wonder of the universe, an answer of one's remaining essence may be found not in the question but in the asking.

The Writer or Musician

I speak of the writer and the musician from where the creator springs if not the dark places the light has had to overcome.

Could the writer speak of love in prose or verse if never to have loved, the musician to play the heartstrings of a sonata if never the rapids of raging heartbeats traveled.

And what of the shadows of man could the writer fashion description, if not for even the briefest of time lived in its underworld hidden from the light to form words appropriate to the verse.

And the musician to play with feeling that moves to tears would it not possible to be if there'd been no exploration of the depths of the heart's expression.

And what of fear, doubt and uncertainty that plague mankind, could the writer speak as he must from the palette of word pictures if not have once lived in the darkness of a broken heart.

For the Birds

We bought a bird feeder, nice one too, not real big but enough for a couple of Sparrows, a Wren and a Chickadee or two.

From the box we couldn't wait to hang it in the backyard just off the patio from our twenty-year-old Linden Tree.

We checked it every minute, sure the birds would find it quickly, but birds being birds had their own agenda and the first day none showed up to feed from the trough we'd hung for their dinner.

The second day went by but not discouraged, they'd certainly show once the word got around of a new feeder in town all stocked with seed of great variety an epicurean treat for the delight of our feathered friends.

The third day we saw some activity and all excited the birds at last had arrived, we dashed to the window for a better look, but it wasn't birds we hurried to see but a bushy tailed squirrel hanging from the feeder below the tree.

*We checked the box again to make sure it said bird
and not squirrel feeder, assured we were resigned
to watch him come and go trying his darnedest
to jump from the tree trunk to the limb where he
perilously hung before falling to the ground, the
feeder too small for him.*

*We'll fix the little guy we thought to move the
feeder far enough he'd not be able to make the
jump, but outsmarted we were as he'd stretched up
from a flower box on the patio railing, there once
again hanging on the bird feeder below the tree five
feet from the ground.*

*So, Mr. Squirrel, he's persistent but must be
dealt with scaring the birds with his presence,
a cardboard hat I made to cover the feeder,
homemade Squirrel Preventer if you will.*

*It worked as we'd hoped, so well in fact I believed I
should patent it, the squirrel content to stay on the
tree to watch the Sparrows, Wren and a Chickadee
or two come to feed.*

*So all was well with the pecking order decided,
the feeder the perch the birds could have, and as
for the squirrel not to be forlorn, a handful of seed
scattered about on the ground especially for him.*

To Speak of Other Things

"The time has come the Walrus said to speak of other things, of shoes and ships and sealing wax and cabbages and kings," Lewis Carrol

And so it was on a cold morning in November the time had come to put life on hold and speak of other things, of fixing a bad knee, procrastination no longer to hide from the pain of surgery, homage to pay to the god of "all things better" at least for one knee parts to replace and a second one to come later.

And so very early before dawn I found myself being prepped for the starring role with the supporting cast of surgeon, nurses and anesthetist, each special in their field to put my mind at ease.

The first act would go quickly with little to remember of the operating room, the stage lights to come up bright as mine were going out to relight in recovery where the second act began, nurses accommodating my every whim.

The last act played out as I knew it would overnight in the hospital bed, nurses coming and going checking this and checking that, dispensing pills through the night into the next day, the surgeon stopping by to view his handiwork with a few assuring words to say.

And so the play ended as it must, goodbyes were said and I was wheeled out where my wife awaited now entrusted to her care, recovery in earnest to begin in the weeks ahead, pain pills to take, ice to apply, rest and walking about, physical therapy to rehabilitate the pain away, healing to begin.

The day would come when the events of surgery I'd elected would sink into the depths of memory to be recollected in conversation of what had been, some glory I suppose in the retelling before once again to fade from consciousness until the day comes again the curtain to rise of the other knee to fix.

The Great Poet

And now it was many days later, more than a hundred or so, the Great Poet was pleased with the verse each day he'd written at last finished he believed but just to be sure he'd call together the kingdom once more to review all he'd written to see if they thought he should write more.

Let's see, he began, the members of the kingdom attentively listened, I began to write of encouragement, new mothers, sons and daughters off to war, the homeless, freedom and those in the healing professions before vowing to write each day one more.

It's my dilemma now whether to declare complete the masterpiece of verse I've written for all the universe to enjoy, he explained to those of the kingdom he gathered around to help him decide.

They laughed, smiled, and grew serious as he reviewed the many subjects of people and events he'd written so diverse, sure to make the reader stop and think about spirit and the oneness of the universe, so much to see and share of life, the serious and absurd, the power of his love reflected for all to see.

So, then the assembly of the kingdom offered the Great Poet advice, why not declare your writing finished for now, we believe you have written quite enough.

And so he agreed feeling he'd completed his mission and now would lay aside the eternal pen to be content each morning to return to the eternal garden of his inspiration to rest on his laurels, but somewhere deep within he knew that one day sooner or later he'd again put pen to paper to create more verses of his unconditional love.

A Spiritual Rosary

- *God is all there is.*
- *I am one with God.*
- *God is Love, I am Love.*
- *God is Peace, I am Peace.*
- *God is Forgiveness, I am Forgiveness.*
- *God is Abundance, I am Abundance.*
- *God is Trust, I am Trust.*
- *God is Joy, I am Joy.*
- *God is Wholeness, I am Wholeness.*
- *God is Oneness, I am Oneness.*
- *God is Truth, I am Truth.*

End notes

The style of poetry is best described as nonconforming rhyming "Free Verse." As for punctuation I've chosen to be as sparse as possible omitting commas in the interest of unimpeded flow of thought.

The following provides background of some of the poems of the people and events of special meaning:

A special relationship with my grandson (Walking Boys) (My Grandson) developed from the time he was a toddler. At about age six, he began telling us we were the greatest grandparents in the whole universe.

Our early wedded lives began in Albuquerque and the Land of Enchantment has continued for more than fifty-five years to hold a special place in our hearts (The Man I Met) (The Jewelry Man) (Ojo Caliente) (Fiesta).

My stepmother, Jean Louise, inspired "She's Louise." At 5 foot 2 inches and 90 pounds she was tender as a twig and tough as an oak, raising six of us kids through some very tough times.

The man at the fence calling the cows was my dad who we thought always had a lot of bull.

My flying and sailing adventures inspired several poems (Morning Flight), (Barnstormer) (Solo) (Lady of the Sea).

"Uncommon Words" was inspired by an unconventional speech teacher at the University of Albuquerque.

Several poems reflect my long harsh winter journey through the wastelands of mental illness (Fall from Grace) (Madness) (Who Am I) and the conflict of the journey to regain the "Truth of Myself" (Veil of Distortion) (New Dawn) (Spiritual Journey) (Spirit Struggle) (Awakening).

I chose to end with "A Spiritual Rosary" a form I adapted from the Catholic tradition of prayer to the Virgin Mary, which best captures my relation to the one God of the universe. I've found it helpful to daily repeat the short aff rmations.

I hope you enjoyed "Reflections of Us" I'd be pleased to hear from you with comments about your favorites as well as the story you'd care to share of your spiritual journey, no matter what path you're on. Contact me at ref ectionsofspirit@gmail.com.

Thomas Himes